NEW JERSEY
Ghost Towns

NEW JERSEY
Ghost Towns

UNCOVERING
THE HIDDEN PAST

PATRICIA A. MARTINELLI

STACKPOLE
BOOKS

Published by
STACKPOLE BOOKS
5067 Ritter Road
Mechanicsburg, PA 17055
www.stackpolebooks.com

Printed in the United States of America

10 9 8 7 6 5 4 3 2 1

FIRST EDITION

Cover photo by Patricia A. Martinelli
Cover design by Wendy Reynolds

Library of Congress Cataloging-in-Publication Data

Martinelli, Patricia A.
    New Jersey ghost towns : uncovering the hidden past / Patricia A.
Martinelli. — 1st ed.
        p. cm.
    Includes bibliographical references.
    ISBN-13: 978-0-8117-0910-1 (pbk.)
    ISBN-10: 0-8117-0910-8 (pbk.)
    1. Ghost towns—New Jersey. 2. New Jersey—History, Local. 3.
Haunted places—New Jersey. I. Title.
    F134.M127 2012
    974.9—dc23
                                        2011028080

To all those who aren't afraid
to wander down the road less taken

CONTENTS

South Jersey

PREFACE

Growing up in South Jersey in the late 1950s, I always enjoyed going out for a Sunday drive with my parents. As we motored past the remnants of tiny towns in the Pine Barrens, my father regaled us with stories of the Jersey Devil and other creatures that haunted the night. When I got older and developed an interest in American history, I came to appreciate the lives of those early settlers who staked their claim on what had to have been a very intimidating environment. Whether they settled in "East Jersey" or "West Jersey," they faced the dangers of wild animals, disease, and starvation daily, not to mention a population of Native Americans who did not always welcome their arrival. Like immigrants to other regions in America, the colonists in New Jersey had the task of physically building their communities from the ground up, learning different trades, growing their food, and surviving without the help of modern-day conveniences, such as computers, cars, and shopping complexes.

As one of the oldest settled states in America, it comes as no surprise that New Jersey has a large number of ghost towns scattered through the mountains, along its rolling plains, and dotting the seashore. A number of different industries, such as glassmaking, whaling, mining, and later the railroads, drew many newcomers to the Garden State. Unfortunately, the decline of these trades often tarnished the bright future of many places. For every town in every county that has been included here, there are very likely at least another half-dozen still waiting to be explored. Some have been reduced by time and neglect to nothing more than cellar foundations that show the outline where houses once stood, inhabited now only by their ghosts. Others have retained a small population that enjoys a tranquil life rarely marred by the noise and chaos found in larger cities and towns. If their populations were less than one thousand, they were included in this book because they no longer enjoy the industry or activity that once existed there. Not all of them were "haunted" in the traditional sense, but in a number of cases, it would be easy to believe that *something* was hovering just out of sight. After all, this is a state that offers everything from a Route 666 and Shades of Death Road to places called Mount Misery, Double Trouble, and Ghost Lake.

This book has been divided into three regions—North Jersey, Central Jersey, and South Jersey—whose people are as diverse as their surroundings. Although these are unofficial designations, most New Jersey residents will passionately dispute the benefits and merits of one area over the other two. Each region has its individual charms and its collective problems, as well as a rich and colorful history. If the pickings seem a little slim in the northern portion of the state, that's only because the area is more heavily populated than the middle and lower sections, and ghost towns are getting increasingly harder to find.

In the past, I have written extensively about the Garden State, but I learned a lot about my home state during the course of my research for this book. Since I believe that history is not static, I was delighted to find that some of the information that has been handed down as true over the years has been recently challenged by dedicated researchers. Their goal is not to discredit the work of early folk historians, but rather to simply set the record a little straighter as new information comes to light. My goal for this book is to provide a glimpse into New Jersey's past with the hope that it will help generate continued interest in some of the forgotten places that molded the history of the state. Perhaps by preserving a record of towns that once thrived within New Jersey, I can inspire others to save what they have now before it, too, is lost to future generations.

I would like to thank all of the terrific people who generously provided advice and assistance with this project, including my editor, Kyle Weaver; assistant editor Brett Keener; my research assistant, Karen Smith; my chief reader, Lois Martinelli; Lt. Carmel Capoferri, New Jersey State Park Police; Janet Worrell, Batsto Citizens Committee, Inc.; Mary Ann Curtis Gonzalez, curator of the Stewart Collection, Rowan University; Supt. Rob Auerenmueller, Wharton State Forest; Steven Schimmel, executive director, Cumberland County Jewish Federation; John W. Carr; Frank and Marie Stubbins; Bob and Judy Moore; Joseph Reinhardt, Indian Mills Historical Society; author George Flemming; Joseph Laufer, Burlington County historian; Frank Powell, Salem County historian; Barbara Price, Gloucester County Historical Society; Rev. William S. Sutton, Plainville United Methodist Church; Jack Jennings, Historical Society of Winslow Township; Michael Bancik, director, Mountainside Public Library; Eric Husta and Linda Gilmore, Atlantic County Division of Parks and Recreation; Kevin Wright, Historic New Bridge Landing Park Commission; Jean Foley, Union County Department of Parks and Community Renewal; David Juliano, director of South Jersey Ghost Research; the Monmouth County Historical Association; and, once again, the dedicated staff of the Vineland Public Library.

North Jersey

NEW BRIDGE

Originally known as Ackerman's Mills, New Bridge in Bergen County became a center of shipping and industry long before America became a country.

History

In 1682, a Swedish explorer named Cornelius Mattyse acquired more than four hundred acres of land along the Hackensack River at Aschatking, a Lenni Lenape word that described the place as "where the river narrows." For generations, the river had provided the tribe with striped bass, herring, and shad, while the land offered game, herbs, and other necessities. The Indians, with no concept of land ownership, probably thought they were humoring the newcomers who wanted to buy the region where they had lived for so many years. Little did they know that the initial trickle of Swedes would soon become a downpour of immigrants from all nations. Thirteen years after he bought the land, Mattyse's property was purchased by David

Ackerman, who in 1713 gave a part of it to his son Johannes and his new bride Jannetje (Lozier) Ackerman. The young couple built a house on Steenrapie Road and a gristmill at Cole's Brook, which was powered by the water from a man-made pond. The mill prospered and a small community known as Ackerman's Mill slowly grew around it.

The construction of a literal "new bridge" across the Hackensack River in 1744 brought settlers from other colonies as well as the Netherlands, England, Scotland, and Scandinavia. The growing town was dubbed New Bridge and soon became a thriving commercial center. Jan and Annetje (Ackerman) Zabriskie purchased the Ackermans' farm and gristmill in 1745 and expanded the mill to accommodate more business from local farmers. In addition to flour and animal feed, New Bridge sent locally mined iron ore by ship to markets in New York and other major cities. Returning ships brought back a variety of goods needed by the townspeople. The Zabriskies apparently made a fortune buying and selling goods during the French and Indian Wars (1756–63) and the town itself prospered for almost fifty years.

In 1771, a "stone dwelling house" with twenty-five acres of land was advertised in the *Pennsylvania Packet* as being for sale in New Bridge. The house stood opposite the Zabriskie home and was considered "very convenient for fishing and fowling." The property was offered very cheaply, possibly because the owners were loyalists who sensed that change was coming and wanted to move away from the town.

The ad suggested that the house would make a good tavern and might make even more money by taking in boarders from the nearby Latin school. Students paid fourteen English pounds a year for the privilege of attending college preparatory courses at the school, which was originally operated by a Mr. Barber. John Wright succeeded Barber as headmaster by 1771. The school was not the only attraction in town, however. Businesses were growing so rapidly that in 1772, Peter De Marest announced that he would drive a "covered waggon" twice a week on Mondays and Fridays from New Bridge to Powles-Hook. The wagon, fitted with curtains and a strong team of horses, would leave town at six o'clock on those mornings.

After war broke out between America and Great Britain, New Bridge became the site of frequent battles, because it was a strategic river crossing for both armies. On November 21, 1776, the British attacked American forces who were trying to dismantle the bridge to prevent enemy access into New York. Four years later, as the war raged on, Gen. George Washington made the Zabriskie home his headquarters; the family, loyal to the British crown, had been forced to flee, and their property was confiscated by American troops. Washington was there to rally the fourteen thousand American soldiers who had gathered in the town. After suffering heavy losses at the hands of the British, the Continental Army was preparing to retreat back into Pennsylvania.

In 1783, when the fighting was finally over, the New Jersey legislature presented the Zabriskies' property to Maj. Gen. Baron Friedrich Wilhelm Augustin von Steuben, a German aristocrat, in recognition of his wartime service to the fledgling United States of America. Von Steuben took possession of forty acres that included a twelve-room mansion, a bake house, smokehouse, coach house, barns, and a garden, along with the gristmill. Five years later, however, the baron sold the property to the Zabriskies' son, John Jr., for twelve hundred English pounds. In the years that followed, the property changed hands many times.

By 1834, the town of New Bridge consisted of a store, a tavern, and a sawmill, as well as about twelve homes. The mill, which had been an integral part of the town's success, remained in operation until 1852, when it burned and was never rebuilt. For a brief time in 1870, investors who built a train station there thought "Cherry Hill" would make an attractive name for the town. When local residents protested that Cherry Hill had no historic significance, the name reverted back to New Bridge by the following year. In 1909, the property was purchased by industrialist Charles W. Bell, who reportedly planned to build a large mill there for the production of cardboard. Two years later, however, Bell transferred his ownership of the land to the American Ink Company, which produced newsprint for area newspapers. The company opened a small factory near the intersection of Main Street and Hackensack Avenue that was still standing in 1952.

The Town Today

New Bridge is now an eighteen-acre park situated within the borough of River Edge. While most of the property is owned by the Bergen County Historical Society, some of the structures, including the Steuben House, are owned and operated by the New Jersey Department of Environmental Protection's Division of Parks and Forestry. The house and one acre of ground were purchased by the state for $9,000 in 1928 and opened as a public museum in 1939. Listed in the New Jersey and National Registers of Historic Places, the Steuben House falls under the supervision of the Historic New Bridge Landing Park Commission, which was created to oversee the maintenance and preservation of New Bridge, which is open to the public.

Directions

From Exit 161 on the Garden State Parkway north, travel about two miles on Route 4 east. Take the exit for Hackensack Avenue north and proceed through two traffic lights, then take the exit for Main Street, River Edge. Turn right onto Main Street. New Bridge Landing is located on the left side of the street.

HIBERNIA

Hibernia in Morris County was a typical mining community operated by European immigrants who first settled in New Jersey in the eighteenth century.

History

Long before the United States was a country, Hibernia attracted a number of European colonists. They weren't interested in the fertile landscape, created by its hills, valleys, mountain streams, and lakes, but what lay below the ground. By the mid-eighteenth century, the newcomers were mining the earth for iron ore, a precious commodity that was used to make stoves, cookware, and other necessities needed by the growing population of the colonies.

A millpond was created in 1765 to provide waterpower for the Hibernia Furnace, which operated between 1767 and 1782. For fifteen years, an iron furnace smelted down the raw ore into rough bars known as "pig iron," which could then be smelted again into iron products. At that time, the Hibernia Mine was run by William Alexander, the son and namesake of the Surveyor General of New Jersey. Ironically, William Alexander Sr., a staunch patriot who had served as a major general during the American Revolution, also claimed the Scottish title of Earl of Stirling. While the British House of Lords refused to acknowledge his claim without proof, Alexander continued to style himself Lord Stirling for the rest of his life.

Workers' housing quickly sprang up around the furnace, where most of the men worked, and construction continued as the mining operation expanded. Under the management of William Jr., Hibernia furnished iron for munitions for the American forces during the Revolutionary War. By the nineteenth century, Morris County was the third-largest producer of iron ore in the United States. The mines at Hibernia remained in operation for more than a century, passing through different owners until they were purchased in the early twentieth century by industrialist Joseph Wharton, founder of the prestigious Wharton School of Business in Philadelphia. Under his ownership, the mines continued to produce high-grade magnetic ore, although the quantity had started to decrease. Wharton, who had amassed vast amounts of land throughout New Jersey beginning in the late 1800s, owned part interest in the Wharton & Northern Railroad, one of two rail lines that ran through the town of about fourteen hundred residents in 1918.

Despite its industrial past, Hibernia was promoted in the early twentieth century as a town with a healthful climate and pure well water that was fed by mountain streams. It reportedly provided all the same advantages as more expensive mountain resorts. Four train lines offered passenger service to the town and a trolley line ran close by. Although it had no bank and no telegraph service at the time, Hibernia did have telephone service. There were two public schools that went to ninth grade, three churches (Catholic, Methodist, and Slavish), and cheap rents. With waterpower from a nearby lake readily available, along with a workforce of several hundred residents, Hibernia was considered to be an ideal location for industry. Existing businesses included the Wharton Steel Company, where twenty men mined iron ore; the M. M. Trimmer lumber mill, which employed twenty men; and the J. V. Ten Eyck lumber mill, where fifteen local men worked. By 1939, all that remained of the ironworks was the millpond.

The Town Today

Only a little more than ninety people lived in Hibernia in 2000, just a fraction of the town's population during the height of its industrial years. A quiet place, Split Rock Road, which runs through the town's reservoir of the same name, has become the topic of much supernatural speculation in recent years. While some locals say mysterious lights have been seen skimming over the reservoir after dark, others claim that the bridge over the waters is haunted by the ghosts of lonely souls who committed suicide—or who may have been murdered—at the isolated spot.

Directions

Take Route 80 north to Route 513 north (Hibernia Avenue). Travel north past White Meadow Lake, through the town of Beach Glen. There, Route 513 turns into Green Pond Road. Keep traveling northeast on Green Pond Road; Hibernia will be the next stop.

IRONIA

The appropriately named Ironia in Morris County was another mining town that once tapped the rich veins of iron ore flowing through the mountainous countryside.

History

Although Ironia was not officially recognized as a town until 1871, the area was first mined in the late 1820s by families who usually worked in isolation on a small scale. There were about ten mines in operation then, run as a secondary source of income by farmers or the owners of the local gristmills and sawmills, including the Smiths, the DeHarts, the Bryants, and the Combs. Their success, however, was enough to attract the attention of wealthy businessmen from nearby Chester and Mine Hill, who decided to create a town in the forest that would house a large number of iron miners to work for their corporations.

In 1869, two of those businessmen, Nathaniel Cooper and Daniel Budd of Chester, persuaded the railroads to extend their lines farther north to Ironia, because rail transport was vital to the success of any mining operation. Working with the Canfields, who owned the nearby Dickerson Mine, they formed three companies to control all phases of production. The Ironia Land and Improvement Company would develop a town, while the Ironia Iron Company and the Ironia Car and Transportation would be responsible for the mining and manufacturing of iron products. After acquiring one thousand acres of land near the railroad, the land company created a plan for the aptly named town of Ironia, which included Main Street, Chester Avenue, and Budd Street. In addition to a railroad station, Main Street became the site of a three-story hotel, a freight building, and a general store. While three houses were initially built for mine workers on Budd Street and on Chester Avenue, few others were constructed after that.

On September 28, 1772, Robert Erskine ran an advertisement in the *New York Gazette* and the *Weekly Mercury*, advising ore carters that anyone who began carrying ore from Hibernia to the Charlotteburg Furnace before October 10 of that year could expect to receive their usual rate of pay of "10s. 6d. New-York money" per ton as long as they carted no less than three tons per week. However, that rate would be reduced to just ten shillings after October 10.

By 1873, America was experiencing an economic depression, and the iron industry was failing everywhere. The owners of all three Ironia companies watched in dismay as their proposed town disintegrated back into the surrounding woodland. While some of the larger mining companies in the region managed to stay in operation for about another ten years, the smaller mines folded. The land company quickly sold the one thousand acres and was dissolved almost immediately afterward.

Dorastus Bryant, a mine owner from the area who also operated a distillery and cider mill, quickly bought the land but instead of using it for industry, he planted peach and apple trees. Park Avenue, which he had opened in the late nineteenth century as an easy route from one part of his property to another, soon became the site of the town's schoolhouse and the Ironia Presbyterian Church. The Evergreen Park House, also owned by the Bryant family, became a popular boardinghouse that attracted many tourists.

Although the small town had not turned into a planned industrial center, it continued to draw visitors who needed a respite from city life well into the mid-1900s. The Peggy Lee in Greenhut Park was a popular hotel that featured a recreation and dance hall. A nudist colony, the Woodland Club, remained in operation from the 1930s through the 1960s, before it was overwhelmed by surrounding development. The housing boom that had started in Ironia in the 1950s also caused most of the local dairy farms to eventually close.

The Town Today

Very little remains of Ironia's mining past. Main Street's hotel and general store, which were still standing in 1902, are gone, and the Woodland Club is now a sportsmen's organization. Visitors to the area can get some idea of what the community once looked like by stopping at the stone and wood building at 1547 Sussex Turnpike that started as the D. L. Bryant Distillery in 1809. Locally renowned for Bryant's Pure Old Cider Brandy, the structure was remodeled into a private residence in 1938. The oldest private home in Ironia, Golden Corner House, was built in 1826, and still stands on the corner of Route 513 and Pleasant Hill Road. One of the few company homes actually built for workers around 1872 is located on Budd Street, while the Community Church on Park Avenue dates from 1907. The houses built in the 1950s that originally sold for about $12,000 are now marketed for about $400,000.

As of this writing, one popular resource into Ironia's past is Bill's Luncheonette, owned and operated by Bill Crowley, whose family moved to the area in the 1940s. The brown, three-story Victorian, with rocking chairs lining its wide front porch, was built in 1860 by D. R. Stryker and served the surrounding community for many years as Stryker's General Store. The Crowleys paid $68 for the business on Route 513, an area known locally as Upper Ironia, when they arrived in town around 1940. Over the years, the building has housed the post office and a Sears, Roebuck outlet, as well as the general store. The current owner, who remembers the days of nickel candy bars and cigarettes that sold for fifteen cents a pack, has written a small booklet titled *Bill Crowley Recalls Stories of Old Ironia*. It is available for purchase at the store where old photographs of Ironia are on display. From the store, it is a short trip to Lower Ironia, which was once the site of the proposed mining community, and some of the town's most historic structures.

Directions

Take Route 206 north into Chester; bear right on Route 513, which will take you directly into Ironia.

HEWITT

The Colonial–era village of Hewitt in Passaic County was another one of the many company towns that sprang up around New Jersey's iron industry in the eighteenth century.

History

Immigrants to the colony of East Jersey quickly discovered that their new homeland was not only filled with many dangers but natural resources that could provide them with a very profitable income. In 1766, German ironmaster Peter Hasenclever brought about five hundred iron workers and their families from his homeland to work at Long Pond Ironworks. The new settlers at the "plantation," as such company towns were then known, not only built an iron furnace and forge but also homes and small shops where they could buy supplies. They also built a dam at Long Pond (known today as Greenwood Lake) on the upper Wanaque River, which provided the waterpower for the furnace and forge. While the men mined and processed the raw iron ore, the women and children worked the land and handled the household chores. The ironworks was so successful that two more furnaces were constructed in the 1860s. The village was named Hewitt and grew to include a church, a combination company store and post office, schoolhouses, and dwellings and outbuildings for the workers and managers. Within twenty years, however, the furnaces shut down because Long Pond could not keep up with the technological advances made by its competition.

By 1918, there were about 250 people living in Hewitt, which then had one public school and three churches—one Baptist, one Catholic, and one Presbyterian. There was no fire department and the nearest bank was located in neighboring Warwick, New York. Hewitt did have a post office from which locals could send money orders and telegraphs or place telephone calls. A station in town for the Susquehanna & Western Railroad saw three passenger trains pull in and four go out every day. Twenty years later, Hewitt's population had dipped slightly. Besides the homes, the town consisted of a white frame Roman Catholic church, a school, and a combination post office and general store.

The Town Today

A number of industrial buildings dating from the eighteenth and nineteenth centuries are still located at the original site, including furnaces, the ruins of the casting house, charging areas, icehouses, and waterwheels. Restoration efforts have saved one waterwheel and stabilized several historic houses. The Old Country Store has been renovated and now houses the Long Pond Ironworks Museum. Members of the Friends of Long Pond Ironworks offer tours of the furnace area and village April through November.

Directions

Hewitt is situated on Route 513, west of the town of West Milford.

ANDOVER

Like other North Jersey communities, Andover in Sussex County started as a mining town but later attracted settlers and visitors because of its healthy and invigorating climate.

History

William Penn and his business associates, who owned most of West Jersey in the seventeenth century, were the first colonists to refer to the semimountainous region in the northern end of the state as Andover. In 1749, William Allen and Joseph Turner bought more than twenty thousand acres there from Penn that included the Andover mine and the village of Andover, where the raw ore was forged into iron products. They operated the mine, forge, and an iron furnace, which was managed for them by Col. John Hackett, for more than ten years. The colonel, who had a reputation as a hard taskmaster, died in 1766.

While that didn't deter eager newcomers from flocking there in search of work, many New York and Philadelphia newspapers often carried announcements of rewards for runaway indentured servants. But missing servants was not the most pressing problem faced by the town's owners. Four years after the colonel's death, the *Pennsylvania Gazette* ran an advertisement that described the property:

> To be LETT for a Term of YEARS Andover Furnace, situate in the County of Sussex, in West New-Jersey, on a Branch of Paquest River, together with an elegant Stone Dwelling-house, Stables, Smith's Shop, Springhouse, and a Number of Outhouses for Workmen; a large Coal-house in which there is at least 7 Week's Stock of Coals for the next Blast; also 5000 acres of well timbered Land to accommodate the Furnace, . . . Scarcely a Mile from the Furnace is an inexhaustible Body of Ore, which may be raised at the easy

Expense of 2s, per Ton, and makes Iron of a superior Quality to any other in America, particularly for the Manufacture of Steel. . . . For the Terms, apply to Mr. ARCHIBALD STEWART, who lives at the said Furnace, or to Messieurs ALLEN and TURNER, in Philadelphia.

Had Allen and Turner made a sufficient fortune by then—enough to allow them to give up the iron mine? Not really. Staunch loyalists, they realized that their comfortable lifestyle was rapidly approaching an end. Sure enough, after the start of the Revolutionary War, the Continental Congress decreed that all production from the Andover Mine was to be reserved for the exclusive use of the American army. To ensure the mine owners' cooperation, Andover Works was placed under the control of the newly formed American government and turned over to Col. Thomas Maybury, who supervised the production of cannon, guns, and ammunition for American troops. Apparently, all work at Andover ceased by 1780, and the property was once more offered for sale or rent.

Nearly fifty years passed before the property was reopened as the Andover Iron Company, owned by Edward Cooper and Abram S. Hewitt. The mine began producing about fifty thousand tons of ore each year, which equaled almost one-third of the production for all of the other mines in the region. Iron from the Andover mine was used to make rifles and ammunition for Northern troops during the Civil War, but like other small North Jersey towns, industry faded out in the years that followed. Instead, Andover became a popular resort town because its location in the lower section of Sussex County kept it virtually malaria-free. By the early twentieth century, it retained a core population of about six hundred residents. But the Delaware, Lackawanna & Western Railroad regularly brought tourists from Hoboken, Paterson, Newark, and New York, as well as Wilkes-Barre and Scranton, Pennsylvania, while the Lehigh & Hudson River Railroad transported people from Boston and other East Coast cities. Neighboring farms provided both residents and visitors with fresh onions, celery, lettuce, and cabbage, while local dairies offered butter, cream, and milk.

Andover had a brush with notoriety in October 1932, when the infamous cat burglar Arthur Barry was arrested there. Barry was a "gentleman thief," who had reportedly stolen more than two million dollars in jewelry from some of New York's wealthiest families, including the Mackays, the Cosdens, and the Livermores. He was so suave that after robbing the Livermores, he not only lit a cigarette for the lady of the house, but at her request, left behind a jeweled pinkie ring that had been a gift from her husband. After Barry's initial capture, he served time at Auburn, a maximum-security prison in Auburn, New York. He escaped in 1929 during a violent prison riot and moved soon afterward to Andover, where he posed as "Mr. Toomer," a traveling windshield-wiper salesman. Soon a suspicious newsdealer, who wondered why Toomer always wanted daily newspapers from Manhattan, led a posse one night to the door of the farmhouse where Barry had been living. The jewel thief was returned to prison and served another fifteen years before he was released.

The Town Today

The location of the once-flourishing Andover Mine is marked today by a twenty-foot bank of shale and huge piles of slag, but the ironmaster's house, dating from the 1760s, still stands. The population still hovers at a little more than six hundred residents, but tourists who enjoy bird-watching, hiking, and antique collecting regularly visit the tiny borough.

Directions

Take U.S. Route 206 north to the ramp onto I-80 west. Take Exit 25 to merge onto U.S. Route 206 north toward Stanhope/Newton.

BRANCHVILLE

Branchville is a picturesque small town in the heart of Sussex County that survived not one but two major disasters in its lifetime.

History

The borough of Branchville, roughly half a mile in size, was officially organized in 1898 from part of Frankford Township; however, the town had been settled almost two centuries earlier by colonists from Connecticut, who were attracted by the readily available water and rich land. The first gristmill was probably established there in the early eighteenth century by William Beemer, but the town didn't really begin to grow until after James Haggerty built a mill there in 1793. Haggerty was one of the region's largest landowners; his son Uzal sold the ground on which the town was later built to Judge John Bell, Joseph Stoll, and Samuel Price. Their surveyors originally laid out the community as an eight-sided polygon resembling an Indian arrowhead. Initially dubbed Brantown, it was rechristened Branchville around 1820 by Samuel Bishop, the district schoolteacher.

By 1844, the tiny community was thriving, with more than thirty homes and a variety of businesses, as well as several mills, a church, and an academy. Ten years later, Virgil Crisman built several water-powered mills that quickly prospered. To protect his power source, Crisman bought an interest in Culver Lake and built the first dam in Branchville. His son Charles, who ran a flour, feed, and buckwheat mill in town, was another farsighted businessman who saw further potential in waterpower. He formed the Branchville Power and Light and Water Company, and built the town's first water-powered electric plant, which provided more than eight hundred local residents with energy and electricity for the princely sum of one dollar a month. A self-taught electrician, Charles was so successful that he soon built similar plants in the neighboring towns of Blairstown, Stanhope, Andover, and Sussex.

With an apparently bright future ahead of it, Branchville attracted the attention of New Jersey's booming railroad industry. Rail service was extended to the town by 1869, allowing local mills and farms to ship products such as grain, vegetables, fruit, pork, beef, and milk to city markets. Forty new homes were built. Branchville, like many other small towns that dotted the lake-covered region, soon attracted tourists from larger cities who arrived six times a day by train. They briefly traded life in their polluted hometowns for the sunshine, fresh air, and clean water offered by Branchville.

Unfortunately, about half the town was destroyed in the Great Fire of 1882, which erupted from a piece of overheated equipment inside the tinderbox known as the Sussex Manufacturing Company's cloth mill. As bucket brigades were forced back by the heat, the Lackawanna Railroad brought the whole fire department from nearby Newton to help combat the rapidly spreading blaze. Although no one was killed or seriously injured, looters ran rampant through town during the confusion. It was later estimated that Branchville had suffered as much as $100,000 in damages.

Residents managed to rebuild their homes quickly, and by 1900, they once again had a working electric plant. Although the town suffered its share of reversals during the Depression, its annual Horse and Cattle Show still managed to draw visitors to the fairgrounds each August. Many of them stayed at the Park Place Hotel, a collection of homes across the street from the fairgrounds that had been converted into one rambling structure. Unfortunately, the aging dam—neglected for generations—broke in 1955, flooding Branchville at almost the exact same time that torrential rains began to fall. Businesses were destroyed, and train rails were washed out. While no lives were lost, it took many years for Branchville to regain even a fraction of its former prosperity.

The Town Today

Even though the train whistle no longer blows, gristmills aren't grinding, and farms are a rarity, Branchville's past is very much in evidence today. Many, if not most, of the original buildings dating to the eighteenth century are still in use as private homes or businesses. The New Jersey State Forestry Department and the National Arbor Day Foundation dubbed the tranquil town "Tree City USA" for planting almost three hundred shade trees in more than forty-five varieties between 2000 and 2010.

Directions

Take Route 139 west to U.S. 1/9 south. Take the U.S. 1/9 truck exit toward I-180/Jersey City/Kearny. Make a slight right turn onto U.S. 1/9 truck. Stay straight to Route 7 west. Go onto the Newark-Jersey City Turnpike/CR-508 west. Merge onto I-280 west. Take the I-80 west exit on the left toward the Delaware Water Gap. Merge onto I-80 express lane west. Merge onto Route 15 north via Exit 34B toward Jefferson/Sparta. Route 15 north becomes U.S. 206/Hampton House Road. Turn right onto Newton Avenue/CR 519. Make a slight left onto Mill Street/CR 519. Turn left onto Main Street/CR 630. If you reach Kemah Lake Road, you've gone too far.

HAINESVILLE

Once a hunting ground of the Minisink Indians, who called themselves "brothers of the wolf," Hainesville eventually became another outpost for colonists in Sussex County.

History

Native Americans once walked the trails here, carrying furs and other goods that they bartered with other tribes who lived along the coast. In 1694, one band of seven hundred Indians reportedly carried seventy thousand pelts through the region. But the Indians were soon pushed out of the area as trading outposts were established by European settlers. One of these outposts was the town of Hainesville, established before the Revolutionary War on one thousand acres purchased from the Gardner Tract by Simon Courtright. The property, originally known as Sandyston, was later sold by Courtright to Peter Hotalen, who then sold it to John Shay. Parshall Howell, who bought Sandyston from Shay in 1825, seemed more determined than his predecessors to help the town grow. He opened the first hotel and a post office in the years that followed, attracting new residents to a place nestled between rolling hills that enjoyed a healthy climate. In 1845, Sandyston was rechristened Hainesville in honor of New Jersey's fourteenth governor, Daniel Haines (1843–51). Born in New York, Haines was a graduate of The College of New Jersey and an attorney. He later served as governor and then as an associate justice to the New Jersey Supreme Court.

By 1918, there were about 350 residents living in Hainesville. While there were no train stations in town, the Lackawanna and Western Railroad stopped just ten miles away in Branchville. Or the locals could cross the Pennsylvania state line into Milford, which was only five miles away, to catch a train. Located on the upper Delaware, Hainesville was promoted as a town with "fine water power" to anyone interested in opening a factory there. At that time, the village had one public school and three churches, two Methodist Episcopal and one Dutch Reformed. Twenty years later, the population hovered at a little more than three hundred people living for the most part in mid-Victorian houses. In the 1930s, the town also was home to one church and an inn dating back to the eighteenth century.

The Town Today

Hainesville is home to the Hidden Acres Golf Course, a nine-hole course that opened in 1977, and the Hainesville Fish and Wildlife Management Area, a bird sanctuary located in a valley between High Point State Park and Stokes State Forest.

Directions

Hainesville lies along CR 645 (Layton-Hainesville Road), which runs parallel to U.S. Route 206. It is adjacent to the Delaware Water Gap National Recreation Area.

WATERLOO

One of the largest restored historic villages in the state of New Jersey is located along the north bank of the scenic Musconetcong River in Sussex County.

History

Waterloo, named for the victory of the Duke of Wellington over Napoleon, started as a small town that grew around a gristmill, probably run by S. T. Smith and Brothers, and a sawmill built on the banks of the Musconetcong River in the early eighteenth century. Following the discovery of veins of iron nearby, the Andover Forge was established here, producing bar iron for shipment to England prior to the American Revolution. The town eventually became home to both the forge and a foundry, where a variety of iron products were produced. During the Revolutionary War, Waterloo's ammunition and cast-iron goods were in great demand by American troops, but the town's fortunes later took a downturn when New Jersey's iron industry began to falter.

The opening of the Morris Canal in 1831 attracted new residents because Waterloo was conveniently located halfway between Jersey City in the east and Phillipsburg in the west. Before long, it had not only a general store and an inn, but a church, blacksmith shop, and mill to grind flour for the townspeople. For many years, the town's location made it an important freight depot. Merchandise was brought from New York by water, and then transported by horse and wagon throughout Sussex and Warren Counties.

Around 1848, a road was constructed from Andover Mine to Waterloo, which allowed mule trains to more easily carry ore that was deposited in the canal boats and then transported to Phillipsburg. The canal was also used for more than thirty years as a major waterway for shipping anthracite coal from Pennsylvania to markets in the east; however, New Jersey's railroad system, which was spreading rapidly throughout the state at that time, soon became a major competitor for the canal's business. Since rail lines like the Lackawanna's Sussex branch and the Morris & Essex didn't have to worry about weather conditions like the canal companies did—the canals could freeze over from December through March—more and more customers began to ship their cargo by train.

Some optimistic businessmen tried to revive the iron industry by reopening old mines just outside of town in the second half of the nineteenth century. In 1872, the Lehigh Iron Company began mining ore on the property of Peter Smith, who lived in Waterloo. West of town, on land purchased from Job Brookfield, the Musconectcong Iron Company of Stanhope opened the Waterloo Mine. For a time, these businesses brought new workers to Waterloo, where a store, hotel, and a blacksmith shop remained open. But life in Waterloo continued to decline steadily along with business on the waterway. By 1900, local residents would have been surprised to see more than one boat a year pass through the canal, which was officially abandoned in 1924 when its charter ended. Times were so hard that by the Great Depression, most people had left town. The only business that stayed open was Smith's Store, a century-old shop heated by a potbelly stove, which offered everything from tea and flour to harnesses and packaged goods. The store, opened in 1831, was still run at that time by a descendant of the Smith family.

In 1939, an old mill of dressed fieldstone was still standing in Waterloo, although it was no longer in use. Once, the canal boats had brought Nova Scotia stone there to be ground and then spread over local cornfields to sweeten the soil. Water still flowed in the old channel, as though waiting for the lock to be opened to let the boats pass through. By that time, the Waterloo Foundry was an abandoned shell that, along with the derelict train station, sheltered hobos traveling in and out of New York City. The transients camped at Waterloo for more than ten years until the train station was moved to Mount Olive, where it was restored and turned into a private residence.

In the 1960s, Percival Leach and Lou Gualandi tackled the unenviable task of preserving Waterloo Village, as they called it. The village eventually became part of New Jersey's Allamuchy Mountain State Park and was operated by the Waterloo Foundation for the Arts, a nonprofit corporation established by Leach and Gualandi, who with the help of a group of volunteers, raised enough funds to restore the buildings and organize programs. By the 1980s, the village had become a popular stop for classical and pop music artists. Unfortunately, after Gualandi died in 1988, Leach became involved in several controversial projects, including the construction of the BASF Corporation headquarters on property that had once belonged to the state park. Violently opposed by many Waterloo Village supporters, the issue ultimately led to Leach's removal from his position with the foundation. The Waterloo board of directors selected a new management team that tried to restore peace, but lost state support in 2003 because of budgetary concerns. As a result, Waterloo Village was shut down in December 2006, but was turned over to the State Division of Parks and Forestry by the following year. As of this writing, the site has only been opened on a limited basis and the buildings have been closed for restoration.

The Town Today

Waterloo Village is the only place on the East Coast where both a canal lock and the remains of an inclined plane can be seen along with the town that grew up around them. The inclined plane was designed to carry canal boats over hills by a system of railroad tracks and cables, overcoming extreme changes in elevation. The town, situated on more than five thousand acres, includes buildings that were moved to the site, such as a 1760s inn and an 1870 Victorian mansion. In addition, it is home to the Canal Village, the Lenape Village, and Rutan Farm. There are several homes and inns, a general store, a sawmill, blacksmith shop, and the Canal Museum.

Directions

Take I-80 to Exit 25 to Route 604 east. Turn onto Waterloo Village Road, which runs parallel to Waterloo Lakes within Allamuchy State Park.

FELTVILLE

The Union County town of Feltville once had a promising future until its "king" abdicated his throne.

History

Peter Willcox, an English colonist from Long Island, was the first to see the potential in what was then an unsettled portion of New Jersey. He built a sawmill at the site around 1736, but the mill was torn down when the settlement at the base of the Orange Mountain began to grow. The expanding town survived several Revolutionary War battles but it wasn't christened Feltville until the mid-nineteenth century. The community was named for David Felt, who had established a stationery business known as Stationers' Hall in Boston in 1815. Ten years later, Felt moved from Boston to New York City, where he produced a variety of office supplies, including almanacs, stationery, business cards, and account books. By the 1830s, Felt was so successful that he opened a branch store in New Orleans. When his mill in New York could not keep up with the demand for his products, the ambitious businessman decided to expand his operation into New Jersey.

Felt bought more than six hundred acres of land from Willcox's descendants and constructed a dam and two large water-powered mills on Blue Brook that were fed by mountain streams. He also built himself a handsome mansion, a church, a school, and a company store, as well as homes for the twenty-four families who worked in his mills. It is very likely that Felt modeled the community after the mill towns that were a familiar sight when he was growing up in New England. He named his new town Feltville, but he was dubbed "King David" by the residents, because he had strict rules for their behavior. Felt required the townspeople to attend church every Sunday and demanded that their children attend class in the one-room schoolhouse. Although the population never grew larger than several hundred people, Feltville remained a bustling industrial town for about fifteen years.

By 1850, about 175 people lived in Feltville, but around that time, Felt suddenly sold the town without warning. Some speculated that family problems caused him to sell, and others thought he was simply ready to retire. Whatever the reason, his successor was a businessman of dubious reputation: S. P. Townsend, the "Sarsaparilla Man." A popular soft drink between the early eighteenth and nineteenth centuries, many Americans believed that sarsaparilla had medicinal properties and sometimes used it to treat syphilis. Townsend, who manufactured his product in Feltville, was well-known for his full-page ads that promoted his drink as a restorative for everything from "excessive indulgence of the passions" to "premature decay and decline," but he had only been in Feltville a few years before the banks foreclosed on the property. Townsend apparently had bilked some of his investors to create an ineffectual patent medicine and couldn't pay the mortgage. The town, almost completely deserted after that, lay dormant for about the next thirty years.

On August 10, 1882, the *New York Times* published an article about the auction held the preceding day at the courthouse in Elizabeth, where more than two dozen speculators bid on acquiring the town and six hundred acres of land. The winner was Warren Ackerman, a developer from Plainfield, who bought it for $11,450 after some fierce bidding from the competition. He renamed the property Glenside Park and transformed it into a summer resort, but as more and more people opted to vacation instead at the Jersey shore, the town's population dwindled once again.

The Town Today

In 1919, the remains of Ackerman's resort town were broken into lots. When the Union County Park Commission was formed two years later, it spent the next decade acquiring parts of Glenside Park and incorporating them into the Watchung Reservation, a recreation area annually used by thousands of local residents and tourists. While a number of the homes, including Felt's mansion, have disappeared, some of the workers' cottages are currently being rented. Other buildings, such as the carriage house, are being restored to create information centers for visitors. The site is open year-round, and special events are scheduled on certain weekends.

Directions

Take U.S. Route 78 to the Watchung Reservation, where Feltville is located on the northern border.

BUTTZVILLE

The small community of Buttzville in Warren County annually attracts tourists for two main reasons: Some can't resist getting their holiday cards postmarked there, while others make the trip to enjoy hot dogs. That's right—hot dogs.

History

On both sides of the road, the ground rolls and dips from shallow valleys into sharp hills. Open fields are blistered with huge rocks, deposited during the movement of glaciers during the Ice Age. While the region was probably settled by European immigrants in the eighteenth century, Buttzville was not officially christened until 1839, when Michael Robert Buttz purchased the property from a miller who had operated a gristmill there for a number of years. Buttz built a hotel in the small town, and several generations of his family continued to live and work there in the years that followed. His son, Charles Wilson Buttz (1837–1913) was two years old when Buttz acquired the property. A second lieutenant in the Union Army during the Civil War, Charles later served as a congressman from South Carolina before retiring to Buttzville, North Dakota.

Mining came to Buttzville in the late nineteenth century when the Pequest Company opened the Pequest furnace there. In 1880, Abram Hewitt, a veteran ironmaster who had served as the mayor of New York, started the operation that produced about fifty tons of iron per day. While operations ran smoothly for many years, Hewitt filed suit in 1898 against the Lehigh & Hudson River Railroad for appropriating land adjacent to the furnace. The railroad was ordered to pay Hewitt $1,112.40 for about ten acres of ground.

Hewitt's son, Peter Cooper Hewitt (1861–1921), was a scientist and inventor who played a key role in the success of the furnace. Educated at Stevens Institute and the Columbia School of Mines, Peter invented a variety of useful tools that were used in daily operations, including evaporators, a mercury vapor lamp, centrifugal machines, a circuit breaker, and a wireless receiver. Peter worked as vice president of the Pequest Company until the furnace was dismantled in 1910. Its closing, however, did not discourage local interest in mining. In 1883, a vein of zinc ore was discovered on the Raub farm between Buttzville and Oxford, so a mine was opened there by the Hartpence brothers of Buttzville, who leased the property with A. J. Swayze of Hope. While the extent of the vein was not known, test pits were sunk to determine if it was worth mining.

By 1917, no members of the Buttz family remained in town, but the hotel built by Michael Buttz was still standing. In the years that followed, the small population occasionally welcomed important visitors, including President Herbert Hoover and baseball great Babe Ruth, who enjoyed trout fishing at nearby Island Park. Buttzville, with its small wood-frame houses and stores, remained virtually unchanged into the late 1930s.

As years passed, another family name became even more closely associated with Buttzville than that of the founder. In 1944, John and Louise Kovalsky opened Hot Dog Johnny's, a small take-out stand on Route 46 that later grew into a larger business a short distance from the original site. The menu remained limited to the basics—hot dogs, fries, and cold drinks—but the business drew its clientele from throughout New Jersey, Pennsylvania, and New York.

The Town Today

Most visitors tend to visit Buttzville to get their holiday envelopes postmarked at the town's small post office, located in a converted gas station of white brick with a blue-tiled roof. Or, they make annual pilgrimages to the Kovalskys' eatery, currently run by their daughter Patricia, which still serves the same basic menu started by her parents and has been cited by the Travel Channel as being one of the most popular roadside stands across the country.

Directions

Buttzville is located on Route 46 just south of Jenny Jump State Park.

Central Jersey

LARISON'S CORNER

Larison's Corner in Hunterdon County reportedly has the distinction of being home to more members of the Rockefeller family than any place in the United States.

History

Amwell Township, established by the English crown in 1708, would become home to a number of villages, including one that was first known as Pleasant Corner, then as Larison's Corner. During the Revolutionary War, an important battle was fought near the town when local minutemen led by Capt. John Schenck successfully ambushed a party of British soldiers. The attack helped to curtail British activity in Hunterdon County at an important time—just before Gen. George Washington and his troops crossed the Delaware on December 25, 1776.

Three years later, George Thompson, an English immigrant, built an inn at the junction of Old York Road and Dutch Lane, but he sold the building and fifty-five acres of ground the following year to Edmond Burke, whose successors included John W. Larison. The inn, which became known as Larison's Corner Tavern, was extremely popular with travelers, who enjoyed drinking and dancing in the large, well-lit downstairs rooms. Upstairs, a Franklin stove heated a small space where men sat nightly to gamble.

By 1811, the name Larison's Corner had become attached to the surrounding town. That same year, the community became the home of the Amwell Academy, which operated from a brownstone attached to St. Andrew's Church. For ninety dollars, Titus and Hannah Quick had deeded the land to Colonel Bishop, George Dilts, David Manners, John Lequear, and John Schenk, who were named trustees for the academy. The school closed its doors in 1830 and lay abandoned until 1870, when Cornelius, Andrew, Katherine, and Mary Jane Larison decided to reopen it as a seminary. Before long, however, their interest in teaching their students was replaced by a family feud over the role of science in the modern world. At that time, huge technological leaps were affecting the course of modern life, often prompting a conservative backlash.

Six years after the Larisons started their seminary, Cornelius and Mary Jane split from their brother and sister and started their own school at the rear of their home. It became known as the Ringoes Academy of Arts and Sciences. Cornelius, formerly a professor of natural science at the University at Lewisburg, Pennsylvania, served as principal. In the 1870s and '80s, he encouraged his students to study geography, which most schools did not include in their curriculum, and took them on frequent field trips. Cornelius wrote several books during his tenure at the school, including the highly original *Geografy: A Text Buk in Fonic Orthografy*, produced in 1885 by the Fonic Publishin Hous in Ringoes.

The Larison's Corner Church was founded as the United First Church of Amwell in 1747. It was primarily attended by German immigrants who could hear services in their native tongue. The present church, erected in 1818, has a cemetery dominated by Rockefellers—so many that John D. Rockefeller thought his ancestor, Johann Peter, was buried there. Rockefeller erected a ten-foot granite monument on the grounds in 1903 that was engraved with the following epitaph:

> In memory of Johann Peter Rockefeller, who came from Germany about the year 1723. Died in 1763. He gave this land for a burial place for his family, its descendants, and his neighbors. This monument erected in the year 1906 by John Davison Rockefeller, a direct descendant.

According to George W. Tine, the Rockefeller family historian, however, Johann is actually buried on a farm in the vicinity of the church.

The Town Today

Life was fairly quiet and mundane in Larison's Corner until an unexpected brush with the supernatural occurred in 2003, when a number of mysterious crop circles were discovered in a field just outside of town. Local residents noted that someone or *something* had created about two dozen irregularly shaped patches ranging from towel-sized to about one hundred feet across in a large field covered in two-foot-tall grass. In every section, the grass was firmly packed down in a north-to-south direction. No one heard anything that night and no tracks—human or otherwise—were discovered leading in or out of the field.

Directions

Larison's Corner is situated at an intersection of U.S. Route 202 and two county roads about twenty-five miles north of Trenton.

RALSTON

John Ralston may not have owned the town, but his influence was so strong that the Hunterdon County community of Roxiticus, listed in both the New Jersey Register of Historic Places and National Register of Historic Places, was later renamed in his honor.

History

Settled by European immigrants in the early eighteenth century, Ralston was originally known by its Indian name of Roxiticus. An Englishman named John Brain is credited with being the first person to build a cabin on what later became Roxiticus Road in 1707. Six years later, John Wills, a clerk to the West Jersey Proprietors, was granted title to more than eight hundred acres there, west of India Brook and north of the Raritan River. While Wills never lived there, his son James is believed to have built the first permanent home in the area in 1724. In the early 1900s, a spiritualist reportedly held séances there in a small room at the back of the house. Later, when the property was known as Knox Farm, it served as an American Legion convalescent home for soldiers who had fought in World War I. In the late 1950s, the elegant two-story house was moved eighteen hundred feet back from Route 24 to a hillside location on Valley View Drive.

During the eighteenth century, the settlement of Roxiticus grew steadily as more colonists were attracted by the area's rich soil and ample water supply. Soon, sections of the forest were cleared for farming and the colonists began to build wider roads rather than continue using the footpaths created by the Native Americans. In 1742, Edmund Martin built the first gristmill and sawmill on the waterways there. Close to a century later, the same gristmill was used to grind local limestone to make cement poured for the Morris Canal, which operated for more than one hundred years. The mill, later known as the Ralston Feed Mill, remained in business until about 1900.

During the Revolutionary War, the mill was run by John Logan, a quartermaster who supplied ground flour and other food to the American army at Jockey Hollow. Logan was such a successful businessman that in 1781, he built a manor house next to the mill, constructing the chimney with bricks imported from England expressly for that purpose. Logan also hired a coach painter from London to paint the first- and second-floor rooms of the house, although the slaves housed on the third floor attic lived in plainer surroundings. Unfortunately, Logan went bankrupt when the war ended and the

Continental Congress failed to pay their bills. He managed not to lose his property, however, after John Ralston, a wealthy merchant from Philadelphia, arrived in 1785.

Ralston not only married Logan's daughter, Margaret, but he allowed the family to remain in their home and kept the mill in operation. In addition, he built a combined mill office and general store where he and his partner, Hugh Nesbitt, conducted business. With improved roads and the growth of the iron industry, new settlers soon flocked to the town. In 1806, the Washington Turnpike (known today as Route 24) became the main highway from Ralston to many major cities. The new highway allowed Ralston and Nesbitt to barter extensively with companies in New York and Augusta, Georgia, for goods that they sold at the general store. Since money was in short supply after the war, they traded iron, peach brandy, applejack, and hats that were shipped by stagecoach in exchange for indigo, molasses, cotton, tobacco, silver buckles, and silk handkerchiefs. In 1893, the general store served as the town's post office and remained in use until 1941.

Ralston built an elegant Federal-style frame house for himself and his bride shortly after their marriage. In 1813, he purchased the neighboring Wills plantation, which was situated on more than four hundred acres, for $14,000. The small farmhouse became home to his daughter Mary Ann and her husband, Hugh Nesbitt, the nephew of Ralston's business partner. In the mid-1800s, the house was dramatically enlarged into a Georgian mansion, with a two-story portico added to the front.

Ralston, who eventually amassed about two thousand acres of property, encouraged others to establish local businesses. In addition to a two-story, wood-frame cotton mill, a fulling mill opened there in the 1850s on Union Schoolhouse Road. There, wool was dyed, spun, and woven with linen into a fabric called "wolsie." The building was destroyed by a flood in 1919 and only the foundation remains visible today. In 1891, the Rockaway Valley Railroad ran through town, crossing Route 24 about one-quarter mile west of the general store. After Ralston's death in 1833, his mansion was purchased by John Wick Ledell and remained in the Ledell family until the 1950s.

Ralston's influence was so strong that local residents began referring to their town by that name, although it was not officially rechristened until the late nineteenth century. Ralston's grandson, John Ralston Nesbitt, who built and operated a gristmill there, was instrumental in changing the community's name. In 1908, Thomas Laughlin purchased the mill and converted it into a distillery where he made Tiger Applejack, also known as Jersey Lightning until the advent of Prohibition. By 1919, all the local mills had closed and farming became the town's main occupation.

The Town Today

Ralston has retained much of its historic charm, thanks to an active preservation effort that has saved many eighteenth- and nineteenth-century homes and buildings. Once a year, the Ralston Historic Association hosts a tour of some of the houses for the general public. The general store is currently open to visitors as a museum between June and October.

Directions

Ringed on all sides by nature preserves, including Schiff, Burnett Brook, and India Brook, Ralston is located west of Mendham on CR 510.

RALSTON HEIGHTS

Ralston Heights in Mercer County was envisioned by one man as New Jersey's version of the Garden of Eden. Unfortunately for him, reality soon took a bite out of that grand plan.

History

Albert Webster Edgerly first conceived his philosophy of Ralstonism in the late nineteenth century. Within a few years, he claimed to have almost a million followers of his "grand movement," which was intended to promote the health and alleged superiority of the Caucasian race. The concept was started as the Ralston Health Club, where members were ranked by degrees from zero to one hundred, moving upward toward enlightenment. They advanced five degrees at a time—sometimes by purchasing a copy of Edgerly's writings, which automatically counted for the required five degrees. Regents were those members who brought newcomers into the fold.

Born in 1852 in Massachusetts to Lucinda Stone and John Foss Edgerly, the founder of Ralstonism graduated from the Boston University School of Law in 1876 and started the Ralston Health Club that same year. Sixteen years later, Edgerly married Edna Reed Boyts in McConnellsville, Pennsylvania, and practiced law in Kansas, Boston, and Washington D.C. In *The Book of General Membership of the Ralston Health Club*, published in 1900, Edgerly explained that Ralston was an acronym for "Regime, Activity, Light, Strength, Temperation, Oxygen and Nature." Edgerly believed his system would allow the Caucasian race to succeed better once it was freed from what he deemed "impurities." He also believed that all non-Caucasian males should be castrated at birth.

In the 1890s, Edgerly bought large tracts of land in the Hopewell Valley. There he built Ralston Heights, a huge gothic castlelike house that was supposed to serve as home to an entire community of members known as Ralstonites. They were to be the first settlers in Ralston, a new community that would be part of his Universal City. Edgerly planned everything to his own specifications. The turreted mansion, which sat at the top of a circular driveway, contained round rooms and a maze of interconnecting hallways. A mysterious garden was walled off from the rest of the property by an eight-foot-high brick fence. The remaining grounds, laid out in a circular pattern, rambled and turned in different directions because Edgerly believed that walking in a straight line sapped vital life energy. He planned that his new city would not only include small farms and lots for private homes, but also seven palaces and a Temple of Ralston. But his proposed community was never built.

Edgerly expected his followers to adhere to strict dietary rules. They were to avoid watermelons, which he claimed were poisonous to Caucasians. The Ralstonites had to maintain a good diet and get a lot of physical exercise, which involved activities like walking exclusively on the balls of their feet and moving in graceful circles. If they followed Edgerly's regime, then they would achieve "personal magnetism," the ability to control the thoughts of other people. Their leader claimed that his ideas for the proper way to walk, talk, bathe, sit, sleep, and have sex were all supported by scientific evidence.

All of Edgerly's beliefs were discussed in eighty-two books that he wrote using the *nom de plume* Edmund Shaftesbury. In addition to discussing diet and exercise, the books offered advice on personal hygiene, artistic deep breathing, facial expressions, and ventriloquism. In addition, young men were advised to participate in probationary marriages with older women. Edgerly, who sold most of his books by mail order, also created his own language called the Adam-Man-Tongue, comprised of an alphabet of thirty-three letters. In 1900, Edgerly partnered with William Danforth, the founder of the Purina Food Company (which subsequently became the Ralston Purina Company), to produce a very successful whole-wheat cereal for both the Ralstonites and the general public.

Edgerly died in 1926, and his widow sold Ralston Heights the following year. Although later owners made some attempts to clean up the property, by the 1990s, it remained an abandoned derelict, the topic of local lore and speculation.

The Town Today

As of this writing, Edgerly's former home and several ruined buildings were still standing on the overgrown property.

Directions

Hopewell Township lies northeast of Washington Crossing State Park off Route 29, which divides New Jersey and Pennsylvania.

FELLOWSHIP FARM

Marxists, socialists, or just plain freethinkers—all once found a home at Fellowship Farm in Middlesex County, where they tried to work together to make a living off the land.

History

The stucco relief carved into the Sam Goldman house, in the case of Fellowship Farm, is the picture that is literally worth a thousand words. Goldman was an artist who created, in the midst of other Art Deco designs, the image of a plainly dressed man and woman staring into the distance, their sleeves rolled up and ready to work. The woman has her hair pulled back into a bun and wears an apron, while the bearded man wields an axe over one shoulder. If they were typical of the residents who first settled Fellowship Farm in 1912, it is not surprising that the utopian anarchist community in North Stelton lasted for more than twenty-five years.

North Stelton, just two miles from the town of Stelton, was selected as the site of Fellowship Farm by a group of German Socialists then living in New York City. In the summer of 1912, they advertised in the *New York Call* that anyone who was tired of the pollution and cramped quarters of city life was welcome to join them in forming a collective to live off the land. Advised by George Littlefield, another freethinker who developed utopian communities throughout the United States, the socialists raised $8,000, which was used by that October to purchase the Letson farm. The property had been recommended to them by the New Jersey State Agricultural Experiment Station, and that winter, a group gathered at the farm to form the core of the Fellowship Farm Cooperative Association. The members met on Thanksgiving Day in the twenty-two-room manor house, an elegant structure with high ceilings and marble fireplace mantles that would serve as their headquarters in the years that followed.

Under their agreement, each member leased and farmed a plot in proportion to the number of shares that were held. They gave the streets of their new home names such as Voltaire, Justice, Brotherhood, and Karl Marx. The fledgling farmers soon learned that they perfectly timed their departure from New York. By 1914, continued social unrest led someone to try to assassinate millionaire industrialist John D. Rockefeller with a bomb. Instead, four people who lived in a tenement were killed, turning public sentiment against anyone who wanted to change the social order.

Unfortunately, most of the former city-dwellers who moved to the farm had little agricultural experience, and as a result, their efforts to grow crops were rarely successful. Some began raising chickens but many continued to commute to jobs in New York and other cities. Community enterprises such as a store and a bus line gradually passed into private control, largely because no one, in the interest of democracy, was willing to delegate full authority to a competent manager. During the Depression, however, the colony established a cooperative garment factory that operated successfully for many years.

Harry Kelly, a socialist from New York affiliated with another radical group, the Ferrer Association, visited his friend Mary Krimont at Fellowship Farm in the summer of 1914. He was very impressed with the community. Even though the land had been acquired collectively, it would be farmed individually. While some members could only afford to lease one acre, others tried their luck with up to four acres at a time. Lots were drawn for the location of the plots and about ten acres were reserved for use as a community park. Since the closest shop was in New Brunswick, four miles away, a cooperative store was started in 1913. After Kelly's glowing reports about Fellowship Farm, the Ferrer Association started a school in neighboring Stelton in 1915. The Fellowship Farm celebrated its twenty-fifth anniversary in 1937, but was dissolved a few years later because of bankruptcy.

The Town Today

While the Goldman house, covered in a variety of reliefs, still stands abandoned on School Street, Fellowship Farm's administration building is used as a civic center where various groups meet and voters cast their ballots at election time.

Directions

From the New Jersey Turnpike north, get on I-95 north, then exit toward CR 527/NJ 18 north. Bear right at the fork and follow the signs for NJ 18 north/U.S. 1/New Brunswick/Princeton/Trenton/Tower Center Boulevard and merge onto CR 527 /NJ 18 north. Bear right toward NJ 27 north/Albany Street/Raritan Avenue; take the ramp onto NJ 27 north/Albany Street/Raritan Avenue. Turn left at Plainfield Avenue to Stelton Road.

RARITAN BAY UNION

The utopian colony of Raritan Bay Union was founded in Middlesex County as a place that promoted equality between men and women.

History

Raritan Bay is situated on Lower New York Bay between Perth Amboy and Staten Island, New York. It was named after the Raritan tribe, a branch of the Lenni Lenape who lived there for centuries in villages, hunting and fishing in the surrounding forests and waterways and gathering shellfish along the shore. Unfortunately, most of the evidence of their lifestyle was destroyed after the arrival of Dutch colonists in the seventeenth century.

In the mid-nineteenth century, Raritan Bay became home to another group whose lifestyle was almost completely erased. In 1858, the Raritan Bay Union was formed on a large parcel of land overlooking the ocean on the north shore of Raritan Bay, about one mile from Perth Amboy. The area had long been known as Eagleswood, because of the large number of eagles who made their home in the surrounding forest. The utopian community was founded by Rebecca Buffam and her husband, Marcus Spring, with some other former members of the North American Phalanx (see page 41), who moved into a cottage built there by a Dr. King, the former owner. Buffam and Spring hoped that the Raritan Bay Union would be more pragmatic than the North

American Phalanx—somewhere between utopian thought and the real world. After their communal hall, or phalanstery, was built, it served as home to a school, the students, and some community members, as well as the kitchen, shops, laundry, and work rooms. Buffam and Spring chose to live nearby in a private residence.

Like the North American Phalanx, residents at the Raritan Bay Union followed the teachings of French socialist Francois Marie Charles Fourier. Its members were socially and politically active and could choose between living in private quarters or communal settings. Among the liberal thinkers who stayed at Raritan Bay Union were Henry David Thoreau, Caroline Kirkland, and Amos Bronson Alcott. Many liberals of that time spoke of equality between the sexes, usually adding a disclaimer that women should continue to dress appropriately and to think and act like the moral centers of humanity, but the Raritan Bay Union seemed to have been a place where true equality was encouraged.

The community was home to a progressive, coeducational boarding school run by Theodore Weld, the husband of abolitionist Angelina Grimke, where girls not only participated in sports, but were encouraged to speak in public and act in plays. Grimke and her sister, Sarah, had been active opponents of slavery in their home state of South Carolina. The Grimke sisters and other noted reformers like Elizabeth Peabody taught at the school before it closed around 1861, about a year after the Raritan Bay Union was disbanded. The colony had been well-financed and well-received, but its original principles based on Fourier's teachings were not followed by all the members. When division set in after just two short years of operation, the experiment came to an end. The phalanstery, however, was later turned into a military school, then a hotel, and finally part of a tile factory before it was abandoned.

The Town Today

Although Raritan Bay Union is now nothing more than a memory, the region itself is known by anglers as a prime fishing spot.

Directions

Take the Garden State Parkway north and exit onto NJ 36 south; turn left at Poole Avenue, and then make a slight right at Florence Avenue. Turn left at Dock Street to reach Raritan Bay.

RARITAN LANDING

Once a bustling riverside port, the remains of Raritan Landing in Middlesex County are now buried beneath Johnson Park in Piscataway.

History

In colonial times, Raritan Landing was the last inland stop on the Raritan River for oceangoing ships that carried away lumber and produce carted into town by local farmers. In return for the goods that were shipped by boat to New York and other far-off ports, more exotic merchandise was brought back to the community and dispersed to local general stores. Raritan Landing grew so renowned as a center of business that it attracted settlers from other colonies. Adolphus Hardenbrook left New York in 1719 and settled in Raritan Landing even before the town had a name. He built a house on a hillside and a warehouse on the riverbank, from which he exported grain and imported other products. Many of the goods that were unloaded at the port by merchants like Hardenbrook were transported to New Brunswick and other smaller communities. By 1740, more than one hundred people lived there.

In 1741, another grain merchant, Cornelius Low, decided to build a sumptuous Georgian mansion that was one of the largest and most expensive homes in the province of East Jersey. It featured a center hall and large, airy rooms that were dramatically different from the Dutch style of architecture that dominated the area at the time. The stone was quarried from different sites and carved into large rectangular blocks. Low reportedly didn't care about the cost because he intended to have the most impressive home in town. The Lows raised five children there, and by 1774, their son Isaac continued to run the family business from New York.

John and Helena Castner ran a general store in the 1750s that stocked some of the goods that were shipped into Raritan Landing. In addition to cloth, shoes, pewter, and stoneware, local residents could select from a variety of tools and household utensils. But within a few years, the Castners and their fellow storekeepers ran short of some supplies as the residents of Raritan Landing chose to boycott British goods. Occupied by English troops early during the Revolutionary War, the town reportedly suffered a lot of damage at the hands of enemy soldiers. Fortunately, the community was rebuilt within a few years after the war ended. By 1825, Raritan Landing was once again filled with a variety of shops and warehouses to serve the needs of local residents and travelers passing through town.

In 1830, the construction of the Delaware & Raritan Canal, followed by the opening of the railroad, started a downward spiral that ultimately destroyed the community, because it was no longer a vital link between the countryside and the outside world. Over the next forty years, Raritan Landing went from serving as an important port to pastureland where local farmers grazed their cows. Although the town was nearly gone, not everyone had forgotten it. After years of research, Piscataway resident Cornelius C. Vermeule created a map of Raritan Landing in 1936 and published his findings in an article for the New Jersey Historical Society.

The Town Today

In 1977, highway construction in Piscataway was delayed when some historic artifacts were discovered beneath the surface of River Road. But it wasn't until 2000 that archaeologists began to uncover a wealth of objects, including musket balls, brass buttons, and bone-handled pocket knives, which offer some clues as to what life was once like in Raritan Landing. Although most of the houses that still lay buried beneath the surface will not be uncovered, the findings were significant enough to generate new interest in preserving the history of the town. Further information on Raritan Landing can be found at the Cornelius Low House on River Road, which serves these days as the Middlesex County Museum, administered by the Middlesex County Cultural and Heritage Commission. The museum, which offers exhibits, workshops, and special events, is listed in the New Jersey Register of Historic Places and the National Register of Historic Places.

Directions

From the New Jersey Turnpike, take Exit 9 toward New Brunswick. Take Route 18 north and then the exit for Highland Park/Route 27 north. Make a left at the traffic light onto River Road. Look for Johnson Park on the left at the first traffic light onto Cedar Lane. The park runs parallel to River Road.

ROOSEVELT

During the Great Depression, the federal government ordered the creation of an experimental town called Roosevelt in Monmouth County, which was meant to give displaced people a second chance at a better life.

History

Initially known as Jersey Homesteads, the town that would later be named Roosevelt was established in 1937 by an act of the New Jersey Legislature. What prompted the state to step in and create its version of a utopian community? It's simple. The Depression had thrown millions of people out of their homes. In response, President Franklin Delano Roosevelt proposed the New Deal, a package of programs designed to help the nation recover from its economic difficulties. Jersey Homesteads was meant to serve as a model for other towns by providing new opportunities for sewing factory workers from the slums of Philadelphia and New York. Although the project garnered support from prominent public figures such as Albert Einstein, labor union representatives were vehemently opposed to it. They protested that such a factory town was a throwback to the early company towns, in which workers had no rights, and the unions would be prevented from successfully negotiating wage increases. Some of Roosevelt's political opponents felt that the project was a costly risk at a time when the nation's economy was too unstable.

Their objections did not prevent the construction of Jersey Homesteads, which started around 1936 after Brown Construction bought a 1,200-acre tract of wooded, rolling farmland in Monmouth County. Before long, 150 homes were built and assigned by lottery to their new owners, who had each contributed $500 to the town's general fund to finance a farm, construction of a women's clothing factory, and other public buildings. Most of the buildings were Bauhaus-style, designed by architect Louis Kahn. The houses were built of cinder blocks, with four to six rooms, flat roofs, and small windows. Although plain in appearance, they were reportedly equipped with all the modern conveniences. The construction company also built a school and cooperative stores, all of which were air-conditioned in the summer and heated with oil in the winter.

The residents organized the Jersey Homesteads Agricultural Association that summer and started a cooperative 414-acre farm, complete with separate units for poultry and dairy. The profits were shared equally among all of the residents, no matter what type of work they performed. The members of the cooperative also started a one-story clothing factory constructed of steel and glass in 1936, which was supposed to help them supplement their farm income. Unfortunately, by January 1937, the factory failed and there was a serious housing shortage. Three years later, the state bought back all of the land and leased the farm cooperative to five local farmers. While the Jersey Homesteads didn't last through World War II, the town's name was changed to Roosevelt in November 1945, in honor of the president, who had died earlier that year.

The Town Today

Roosevelt, with a population of about nine hundred people, is listed in both the New Jersey Register of Historic Places and the National

Register of Historic Places. It was the subject of a documentary, *Roosevelt, New Jersey: Visions of Utopia*, filmed in 1983.

Directions

Take Route 195 north through Imlaystown to CR 524 east to Roosevelt Street, which runs through the Assunpink Wildlife Management Area. Halfway through, the street turns into Roosevelt Avenue and runs directly into the town.

NORTH AMERICAN PHALANX

The North American Phalanx was a utopian experiment in Monmouth County designed to prove that people would thrive better in a communal setting rather than living individual lives.

History

The philosophies of Francois Marie Charles Fourier of France drew a lot of favorable attention in America in the mid-nineteenth century—a time when many people sought alternatives to the existing social structure. His work had been interpreted by Albert Brisbane, a New Yorker who had studied Fourier's social theories on a trip to France. Fourier proposed the concept of the *phalanstére* (phalanstery), a single structure in which individuals would live a communal lifestyle. He felt that individualism created an imperfect and immoral social structure and that a cooperative society was the only way humanity could achieve its full potential. *Phalanx*, taken from the Greek language, meant a "strong union."

In 1839, Brisbane organized the Fourierist Society in New York and the following year published *The Social Destiny of Man*, a book based on Fourier's concepts. He made a convert of Horace Greeley, the powerful publisher and editor of the *New York Daily Tribune*, who became an avid supporter of his cause. In 1843, Brisbane began publishing *The Phalanx*, a journal devoted to Fourierist philosophies, and advocated the formation of a phalanx in the United States.

Shortly afterward, Charles Sears and Nathan Starks formed the North American Phalanx in Albany, New York. When local residents failed to respond favorably to the idea of a utopian community in their midst, the two men decided to start over in New Jersey. They created a commission that received financial support from people like Greeley and Park Goodwin. After raising $14,000, the commission purchased 673 acres of land in Monmouth County from Hendrick Longstreet and Daniel Holmes in 1844. Sears later served at different times as the community's director, secretary, and president and also kept a detailed record of its first nine years of operation.

Six families originally settled at the site, but since living standards at the Phalanx were better than most people enjoyed elsewhere at that time, a stream of workers trickled steadily in from throughout the Northeast in the years that followed. The associates, as they were known, were primarily from the lower and middle economic classes and were selected for their skills such as carpentry and husbandry. But the Phalanx also attracted doctors, lawyers, scientists, and writers. Prospective members were required to live there for thirty days before the rest of the community decided if they should be offered memberships. Wages were based on the type of the work they performed for a week, which ran anywhere from sixty to more than one hundred hours. Women not only held management positions but were expected to share in the physical labor, which shocked the residents of surrounding communities. It was even more shocking when they showed up in neighboring towns wearing the scandalous baggy pants called bloomers, named for the feminist Amelia Bloomer. The cost of living at the Phalanx was about $2 per week for room and board. The community's population usually never exceeded 150 members, although Fourier's original plan called for 1,620 people living together in the phalanstery. While private property was allowed, the members shared activities such as cooking, child-rearing, and dining.

The residents first lived in two farmhouses, but in 1847, the construction of a three-story addition joined them together into one large structure that contained living quarters, a kitchen and dining room, and community rooms. In addition, the grounds included a nursery, a school, farm buildings, and carpenter shops, as well as forges, a man-made pond, and a landscaped garden. A large portion of land was set aside for fruit growing; peach, apple, and pear trees were planted along with grapes and quince. Despite a promising start, the members began to argue over a variety of issues, including abolition and women's rights. Religion also became a problem. Since the beliefs practiced there included Judaism and several denominations of Christianity, including Presbyterianism and Swedenborgianism, many members were offended by one man's attempt to have the whole community adopt just one faith. Many of them were also unhappy with the minimal wages they received.

In 1853, a number of members left because of these disputes. After a fire destroyed a number of buildings in September 1854, the group's insurance company went bankrupt and the remaining community members were not prepared to accept the fact that they had suffered about $10,000 in damages. By the following year, they voted to sell what remained of the property. One resident, John Bucklin, remained and ran a cannery operation there until his death. His descendants retained ownership of part of the property, including the phalanstery, until 1944. Thomas Guest and John Angell, two other former members, bought another portion of the property when the community was disbanded. New Jersey's North American Phalanx was officially dissolved on January 1, 1857, but the concept lived on. In the foreword of a book titled *The North American Phalanx, an Historical and Descriptive Sketch*, written by Sears in 1886, Edward Howland states that the ideas established there would fuel a phalanx that he and a new group planned to establish in Mexico.

The Town Today

A fire in November 1972 claimed the phalanstery, leaving just two cottages from the community that are currently private homes. One of them, built around 1851, belonged to Marcus Spring and his wife, Rebecca Buffam, who later founded the Raritan Bay Union, which also operated according to Fourier's teachings. Besides these two buildings, all that remains of the community is a roadside marker that offers a brief history of the North American Phalanx and its years of operation.

Directions

To get to Red Bank, take the Garden State Parkway north to Route 520, then go north on Route 35. The North American Phalanx was located four miles west of Red Bank.

TOPANEMUS

Large numbers of Scottish immigrants, who built towns like Topanemus in Monmouth County, were among the first permanent settlers to New Jersey in the seventeenth century.

History

By 1684, half of the twenty-four East Jersey Proprietors were Scottish Quakers, who actively encouraged their countrymen to migrate to the New World to find religious freedom. They often offered each family of settlers five hundred acres of fertile farmland that had been purchased from the Lenni Lenape. John Reid, a Scottish Quaker from Perth Amboy who served as the first surveyor-general of East Jersey, was probably the one who pointed some of the newcomers toward the region that would become home to the neighboring towns of Wickatunck and Topanemus in 1688. The name Topanemus was an Indian word that means "an elk drinking from a brook that flows from a spring."

The immigrants quickly established a Quaker meetinghouse and cemetery on what later became Topanemus Road on one-and-a-half acres of ground donated by Thomas Boel. George Keith, an influential member of the Quaker community who was appointed surveyor-general for East Jersey in 1684, settled near the town and was active in meetings there. Keith was a vocal opponent of slavery, but when

Quaker leaders did not agree quickly enough with his opinions, he converted to the Church of England. By the early 1700s, Keith had persuaded many Topanemus residents to his point of view, and the meetinghouse became an Episcopal church. Elizabeth Clark, the wife of William Clark, was the first person to be buried in the cemetery there in 1693. Up until 1867, more than one hundred local residents were laid to rest there, including many important figures such as Reid; Col. John Anderson, president of His Majesty's Council for the Province of East Jersey; and Thomas Warne, a proprietor of East Jersey.

The Town Today

While the town has become little more than a memory, the Topanemus Preservation Committee was formed in 1967 to protect the cemetery on Topanemus Road, since it is the last link to what once stood there. Unfortunately, the isolated cemetery has frequently been the target of vandals, who destroyed headstones and dug up at least three graves over the years. Although the committee is no longer active, the Marlboro Township Historic Commission and local scout groups have taken an interest in marking and maintaining the site. In 2002, Boy Scout Troop 155 of Freehold Township restored the cemetery grounds while Troop 86 of Marlboro Township cleared a path to the site.

Directions

The cemetery is located 3.5 miles north of the Freehold business district and 1,300 feet west of Route 18. It is bound by Julian Way at the north, Coltsbrook Road at the east, David Court at the south, and Harness Lane at the west. There is an access path three hundred feet northeast of the intersection of Topanemus Road and Weathervane Way that is marked by a small blue sign. The cemetery covers the top of the hill but is difficult to locate because it is surrounded by a housing development.

HARLINGEN AND BELLE MEAD

Somerset County is home to the towns of Harlingen and Belle Mead, which up until the late nineteenth century were considered one community.

History

Harlingen was settled by Dutch immigrants in the early eighteenth century. In 1727, a Dutch Reformed church was built there, but the congregation soon found itself embroiled in a dispute over governance of the church when their minister got involved in the split between traditionalists and the American party. In the nineteenth century, the town was briefly a stop on the Mercer & Somerset Railway.

Plainville, a bucolic farm area, was part of Harlingen up until about 1875. At that time, a land speculator from New York named Vanaken bought many of the local farms and decided to turn the tract into a city that bore his name. Vanaken laid out streets and lots for homes and built a railroad station that included a restaurant on the first floor. Unfortunately, his finances were not strong enough to support the weight of his plans, so he was eventually forced to sell the property to U.S. Senator John R. McPherson, who reportedly changed the name of the town from Vanaken to Belle Mead for his daughter, Edna Belle Meade McPherson.

In 1901, Belle Mead became famous for a line of candies known as Belle Mead Sweets. The business was started by two brothers, John and Harry Muirheid, who apparently had a fondness for chocolates. The small plant featured glass partitions through which visitors could watch the candies being made. Since Belle Mead was so small at the time, most of the employees were women who commuted from the neighboring town of Hopewell. The business grew so quickly that after four years, the Muirheads relocated, first to Hopewell and then to a larger factory in Trenton.

Between the late 1700s and late 1800s, numerous travelers frequented Woods Tavern in Belle Mead. It was also the stomping grounds for political figures such as Horace Greeley, who spoke there in 1872 when he decided to run for president of the United States. The tavern burned down in 1932. The train station, which was built around 1913, was torn down eight years later. Belle Mead was home to James Baldwin, the author and civil rights advocate, who lived there in the early 1940s.

In 1904, the Hillsborough & Montgomery Telephone Company extended service to both Harlingen and Belle Mead, probably because most of the corporate officers lived in those towns. The telephone company remained in business for the next ten years. The following year, Harlingen farmers formed a Vigilant Association to help one another protect their livestock from theft. The organization remained active for about thirty years.

In 1910, Dr. John Joseph Kindred started the Belle Mead Farm Colony and Sanatorium as a place to treat victims of both mental illness and addiction. He wanted to make his patients comfortable in peaceful surroundings to increase their chances of finding a cure. Kindred supervised the facility until his death in the 1920s. His son, Dr. John Cramer Kindred, continued his work for the next thirty years. In 1951, Kindred's brother-in-law, Dr. Russell Neff Carrier, joined the staff as medical director, and five years later, he bought the facility. By the 1960s, he had expanded the clinic to provide additional services for a broader range of patients.

The Town Today

The Harlingen Dutch Reformed Church still plays an active role in the town of Harlingen. The Carrier Clinic in Belle Mead added a community service program to encourage local students to volunteer in their hometown and has become affiliated with other agencies to promote new ideas on caring for victims of mental illness and addiction.

Directions

Both Harlingen and Belle Mead are located on Route 206 just north of Princeton.

MILLSTONE

Many Dutch settlers, seeking to escape the British influx into New York City, made their homes in Millstone in Somerset County in the early eighteenth century.

History

A large settlement of Lenni Lenape apparently lived along the Millstone River, near the region that would later be known as Millstone. One of the last remnants of their presence is believed to be an Indian mortar used for grinding corn that was discovered on the Van Doren farm. The stone was later moved to the front of the Hillsborough Dutch Reformed Church and a nearby plaque stated that an Indian village once stood "one thousand feet south of the Church." Many local residents believe that the village was the same one referred to as the "Hunters' Wigwam" in the deed and bill of sale given to Lady Elizabeth Carteret in 1631.

In 1688, Capt. Clement Plumstead purchased the tract that would become the site of Millstone. Two years later, a number of Quakers moved to the area, and within a few years, they were followed by many Dutch families who had been displaced by the British in New York City. Like other groups, the Dutch were attracted by the idea of religious freedom promoted by the New Jersey proprietors and by the rich farmland that was readily available. While the Dutch remained the dominant ethnic group for many years, they were later followed by Scottish, German, and English settlers. In 1760, the Millstone Dutch joined the Presbyterians and erected a church on land northeast of the present Dutch Reformed Church.

Around 1738, the county seat was moved from Six Mile Run to the town, which became known as Somerset Courthouse. The county courthouse and the jail were located near the river. Fifty years later, Governor William Livingston established the Supreme Court there. By that time, Somerset Courthouse was an active town, filled with shops and tradespeople, as well as two churches and two taverns. In 1774, colonial leaders established the County Committee of Correspondence there to disseminate information about growing resistance to English rule that was spreading through the colonies. Two years later, the Eastern New Jersey Treasury was moved to the town to protect it from the British.

Somerset Courthouse was strategically located at the intersection of roads that ran between North Jersey and Princeton and between West Jersey and New Brunswick. As a result, it was the site of many battles during the Revolutionary War. At different times between 1776 and 1782, the town was occupied by American, British, Hessian, Loyalist, and French forces. In 1777, after defeating the British at Trenton and Princeton, Gen. George Washington marched his troops along the Millstone River toward Somerset Courthouse. On a cold January night, about three thousand American soldiers entered the town that had just been deserted by the enemy. The Americans camped in Somerset Courthouse and were warmly received by supporters like Rev. Christian Frederick Foering, pastor of the Dutch Reformed Church, who provided them with food and medical attention. Washington stayed overnight at the Van Doren house, which still stands in Millstone's historic district. Afterward, American forces maintained a post in Somerset Courthouse, later capturing a small contingent of British soldiers who had raided New Brunswick for provisions during what would become known as the Battle of Millstone.

By the following year, American military field hospitals were established at Somerset Courthouse, because the fighting was so fierce in the region. The courthouse, the Presbyterian and Reformed churches, and three barns were commandeered for medical use. In October 1779, the British, commanded by Col. John Simcoe, wreaked their revenge on the town by burning the jail, the courthouse, and several local homes. Simcoe's tactics, however, only resulted in his capture near New Brunswick after local militiamen saw the flames. In 1780, Queens College (later Rutgers University) was temporarily relocated to Somerset Courthouse after the British decimated New Brunswick during their occupation of the town. When the war ended, the county seat was relocated to Somerville because the courthouse had been destroyed by the British.

In the 1830s, the Delaware & Raritan Canal (D&R) was built along the Millstone River, turning the town, now becoming known as Millstone, into a trading center for produce, grain, and cattle from local farms. Four large warehouses were constructed that were able to store up to one hundred thousand bushels of grain at a time. A hotel, grocery store, and other shops and businesses were established to support the town's increasing population and the number of visitors who arrived there. In 1860, a one-room, brick schoolhouse was built in the village. Around that time, the D&R Canal annually saw about 1,400 boats go through town, bearing close to two million tons of freight. Many of them carried coal from Pennsylvania to New York City in the 1860s and 1870s. Although Millstone briefly was home to a railroad station in the 1870s, the Mercer & Somerset Railway discontinued that line after about ten years. As with many small towns, however, the railroad had displaced the canal as the primary means of transportation in America, and the D&R lost much of its business by the turn of the twentieth century. Somerset Courthouse was officially rechristened Millstone and incorporated as a borough in 1894.

The Town Today

Millstone is known as the smallest town in Somerset County. Its population rose to a height of more than seven hundred people in the 1970s, but currently stands at about four hundred. Many of the residents still occupy houses that date to the early eighteenth century, while others live in Italianate homes, a style popular in the second half of the nineteenth century. In their midst sits the Bachman Wilson House built in 1956, a 3,200-square-foot Usonion, or ranch style, house designed by Frank Lloyd Wright for Gloria Bachman and Abraham Wilson. The structure is typical of Wright, featuring an open floor plan and a glass wall, set in the heart of two acres. As of this writing, plans have been made by the current owners, architects Sharon and Lawrence Tarantino, to relocate the three-bedroom, four-and-a-half bath house to Sagaponac, New York (more commonly known as the Hamptons), because repeated flooding is damaging the structure in its current location.

The one-room schoolhouse remained open until about 1940 and has since been restored as the municipal building, home to local government offices. The Old Millstone Forge on North River Street, which remained in operation until the last blacksmith died in 1979, is now a museum run by the Millstone Forge Association. The Delaware & Raritan Canal was purchased in 1974 by the New Jersey Department of Environment Protection's Division of Parks and Forestry, which still operates the site as a state park today.

Directions

Millstone is located on CR 533, just west of the D&R Canal State Park and south of the Central Jersey Regional Airport.

POTTERSVILLE

Pottersville is a bucolic town in Somerset County whose fortune rose and fell with the peach crops.

History

Pottersville was originally known as Lamington and later as Potter's Mills. Several mills were built on the Black River by the mid-eighteenth century, producing everything from flour to woven wool goods. One of the first was built and operated by William Willet, who later built a second mill close by. Willet sold goods to the Continental Army during the Revolutionary War. Like many business owners, however, he was ruined when the Continental Congress was unable to pay its bills, because the newly minted American money became worthless by 1780. Three years later, he was forced to sell his mills to Serrin Potter, who renamed the town Potter's Mills, then Pottersville. Generations of the Potter family lived in the community in the years that followed.

By the late nineteenth century, the fertile region was producing each year more than two hundred thousand baskets of peaches, which were shipped by wagon to towns throughout New Jersey and Pennsylvania. Encouraged by the success of the peach industry, the Rockaway Valley Railroad built a spur to Pottersville in 1888 and ran excursion trains out to the town's scenic Black River Falls. The falls were actually three smaller spills that combined to cascade about fifty feet down a mountainous ravine. An amusement park, with a dance pavilion, merry-go-round, refreshment stands, and picnic grounds soon grew around the falls, attracting visitors from North Jersey who often stayed at the Pottersville Hotel. Unfortunately, when the peach crops failed, the railroad discontinued service to the town. The park lost a lot of business in the years that followed, but remained open until about 1920. There were several attempts to mine iron ore between Pottersville and Hewitt, but they were far from successful.

The Town Today

Pottersville is the site of an annual antique show that celebrated its fiftieth anniversary in 2003. Although the town is home to the Purnell School, a private all-female boarding school, Pottersville's permanent population remains at just a little more than three hundred residents. The falls continue to attract many tourists, who enjoy hiking through the surrounding forest. One of the town's most famous residents was Harriet Adams (1893–1982), who authored the still-popular Nancy Drew series of books.

Directions

Located on CR 512, just west of Route 206, Pottersville is situated a few miles south of Hacklebarney State Park. The falls are located north of town.

South Jersey

AMATOL

In their rush to get to the glitzy casinos of Atlantic City, most people just drive right by the remains of Amatol, once one of the most potentially explosive towns in Atlantic County.

History

The United States entered World War I on April 6, 1917, one year before the end of the four-year conflict that saw old empires crumble and new ones rise. With the threat of war no longer a distant problem, the American government decided to build bomb factories throughout the country to make sure their troops were adequately armed during that war and any future engagements. Since such facilities were unlikely to be welcomed in most towns and they couldn't be run without employees, authorities decided that if they couldn't bring the bombs to the people, they would bring the people to the bombs. As a result, officials ordered the mass construction of whole communities around the factories—towns like Amatol, situated just a few miles west of Atlantic City, "the Queen of Resorts."

Although little physical evidence remains today, Amatol was once considered one of the larger "war cities" built in America for the U.S. Ordnance Department after World War I. Designed by Clinton MacKenzie, an architect from New York, Amatol was constructed in 1918 by the Atlantic Loading Company, with space for twenty-five thousand residents. At the time the project was proposed, residents of nearby Hammonton were outraged. According to the March 9, 1918, issue of the *South Jersey Republican*, the townspeople were "stirred up" at the thought of having a munitions site just four miles from their door. Their negative reaction, however, had no impact on the proposed project.

Amatol, named for the volatile chemical used in making the bombs, may have been considered to be a temporary town, but the government knew that it was important to provide all the amenities to lure workers there. Initially, makeshift barracks and some mess halls were erected for the men employed to clear the land and build several miles of railroad tracks to facilitate transportation of the very special cargo that would be produced in Amatol. When that phase was complete, the crews started work in March 1918 on the homes and buildings at the six-thousand-acre site that would eventually comprise the town.

Housing was built two miles away from the plant to reduce the danger of any residents being killed in an accidental explosion—a lesson that had been learned through hard experience at other places. MacKenzie's plans included two- and three-room cottages, small houses, and apartments for about seven thousand people, as well as separate dormitories for the unmarried men and women. In addition, the government built a variety of stores, a theater that seated 750 people, and an assembly and dance hall, along with an eight-room school, a church, and a firehouse. Plans also included a huge cafeteria with a bakery and a butcher shop and a full hospital to care for the residents' medical needs. Although the population never reached the twenty-five thousand mark that MacKenzie anticipated, about ten thousand residents moved in that March even though construction had just begun on the site.

Workers at the munitions plant produced shells ranging from 75-mm to hand grenades. The shells were filled with amatol, which was made from a mix of ammonium nitrate and TNT. Although TNT was more stable, amatol was cheaper and easier to produce and, as a result, used more often in munitions production. The Amatol plant produced about sixty thousand shells a day—that is, until the armistice was declared on November 11, 1918. With the war over, the number declined dramatically as the workers left to seek other employment. Even though production declined, the factory made and shipped ammunition through the early 1920s, when demand finally ceased.

The Town Today

A large white two-story wooden structure on the Black Horse Pike, once the home of Troop A of the New Jersey State Police, and several small homes and some foundations are the only buildings marking the location where Amatol once stood. As of this writing, Mullica Township officials were trying to start a movement to preserve the site.

Directions

Amatol was built along Route 30 about four miles southeast of Hammonton.

BATSTO

Once a thriving industrial town, Batsto is now a state-owned historic site in the heart of the Pine Barrens in Atlantic County.

History

The vast forest known as the New Jersey Pine Barrens, broken only by a network of waterways and open fields, once dominated the landscape of southern New Jersey. The majestic trees sheltered wildlife and plants that provided sustenance to the Lenni Lenape who lived within the region. The tribes, however, were quickly pushed aside by European immigrants in the eighteenth century. These newcomers had other uses in mind for the tall trees, which were rapidly converted into lumber for homes and charcoal to power the forges and furnaces that produced iron.

One of the places they settled was Batsto, also spelled "Batstow" or "Batstowe" on early maps, which means "bathing place," although no one is certain how the name originated. In 1758, part of the land that later would become the town was owned by a land speculator named John Munrow, who had received it as a grant from the New Jersey proprietors. Another portion, known as Whitcomb Manor, belonged to Israel Pemberton, a wealthy Quaker from Philadelphia. Charles Read, a Burlington attorney and entrepreneur who later became a New Jersey Supreme Court judge, bought Munrow's land in 1765 and then purchased Pemberton's estate. The following year, Read built what many consider to be the first iron furnace in the Pine Barrens on the banks of the Batsto River. A small village quickly grew around the furnace, populated by the workers and their families.

With easy access by boat to most of the major ports on the eastern seaboard, Batsto's iron industry prospered. Thousands of acres of the surrounding forest were sacrificed to make charcoal in huge kilns, used to fuel the furnace, while the river was dammed to create a lake that was harnessed as a source of power. Bog iron was readily available in local waterways and was the primary ingredient in pig iron, crude bars that were later resmelted to create cast iron pots, pans, water pipes, and ship fittings. The bars were called pig iron because the molten iron, which would flow from a main trench into smaller side trenches, resembled piglets feeding from their mother.

Read and his business partners, Richard Westcott, John Cooper, Walter Franklin, John Wilson, and Reuben Haines, continued to purchase large tracts throughout the region, but only two years after starting the Batsto furnace, Read was forced to sell out his shares to his partners because of financial problems that made it necessary for him to flee the country. Around 1770, John Cox and Charles Thompson bought full rights to the iron furnace, where they produced munitions and other supplies for American troops during the Revolutionary War. Cox, who had previously served on the Committee of Public Safety, was appointed a colonel during the Revolutionary War. He shored up the defenses along the Mullica River and organized supply lines to Washington's troops at Valley Forge. Some historians believe that the battle at nearby Chestnut Neck was fought because the British were frustrated when they couldn't make their way inland to burn down Batsto's ironworks.

Cox sold the property to Thomas Mayberry of Mt. Holly in 1778, who then sold it the following year to Joseph Ball, who had previously served as a bombardier during the war. An ardent patriot, Ball also produced munitions for American forces. In 1781, his uncle, Col. William Richards, became manager of the ironworks, and three years later, he acquired full ownership of the furnace. Richards, born in 1739 in Pennsylvania, had learned the iron trade as a young man and had previously worked for Cox at Batsto. In 1784, Richards and his wife, Mary Patrick, moved into the mansion, where they raised their eleven children. After Mary died, Richards married Margaretta Wood, who later bore eight children.

When Richards retired in 1809, his son, Jesse, assumed management of Batsto. During Jesse's tenure, the iron furnace reached its peak, producing firebacks, waterpipe, fencing, and other cast iron objects. It is believed the village at that time grew to approximately seventy-five houses, which accommodated a population of close to four hundred people. European immigrants, attracted by the prospect of new opportunities, flocked to the town from countries such as Great Britain, Ireland, France, and Germany. In addition to working in the iron furnace, the villagers could find employment in two sawmills, making bricks, building ships, making charcoal, and operating a lime kiln. A number of the buildings at Batsto, including a gristmill, general store, and post office, were constructed during Jesse Richards's years of ownership. Jesse also expanded the mansion on the hill, where he and his wife, Sarah, raised their six children.

Unfortunately for Jesse, the iron industry in South Jersey declined in the years that followed. The bog iron, once readily available, had been completely stripped from local streams and rivers. The discovery of anthracite coal in Pennsylvania meant that the forest was no longer needed by ironmakers as a fuel supply, so competition was springing up in other parts of the country. In an effort to keep his workers employed, Jesse built a glassworks around 1847, which operated successfully for about twenty years. The glassworks primarily made window glass and panes for lighting fixtures, two products that were in great demand. After Jesse died in 1854, his sons Thomas and Jesse Jr. assumed control of the property, but mismanagement and a major fire, which destroyed seventeen workers' houses and the remains of the gristmill, forced them to put the property up for sale in 1874.

Two years later, Batsto was purchased by Joseph Wharton of Philadelphia at a Masters Sale. Wharton was an enterprising businessman who invested heavily in property throughout New Jersey. Although Wharton, his wife Anna, and his three daughters never lived at Batsto full-time, he spent about $40,000 to make the owners' mansion comfortable for his family. He renovated it into the popular Italianate style, adding a tower that housed a huge tank to supply water to the house. Wharton had initially purchased dozens of abandoned industrial towns like Batsto with the idea of pumping fresh water from the Pine Barrens to Philadelphia. But he was soon thwarted by state legislation that prohibited such export.

Wharton hired different managers to look after Batsto when he was not in residence. One of his most trusted advisors was Elias Wright, who had served as a brigadier general during the Civil War. Wright was initially responsible for surveying the ninety-two thousand acres of ground that Wharton eventually owned, and he refurbished a number of the buildings, including the sawmill and gristmill, for daily use.

Only about fifty residents lived at Batsto by the time Wharton purchased the property. Although times were difficult, they stayed on primarily because Batsto had been their family home for generations. Wharton offered them new employment opportunities in his sawmill and in the growing cranberry industry. A town census showed that among the residents in 1890 was David Coleman, who had served in the Civil War from August 1864 until June 1865 as a private in Company A, 3rd New Jersey Cavalry. Coleman, who had been shot in the left leg during the war, was listed as disabled. John Moore was another Batsto veteran who had served from November 1861 to July 1865 in the Civil War. A private in Company G, 4th New Jersey Infantry, Moore reportedly spent nine weeks in Libby Prison in Richmond, Virginia.

After Wharton died in 1909, the property was managed for the family by the Girard Trust of Philadelphia. It fell into disuse, but in 1954, it was purchased by the state of New Jersey for about $2 million. At that time, environmental groups and local historical societies had banded together and persuaded state officials that the property was worth preserving. The site, named after its final owner, was opened to the public in the 1960s after the Batsto Citizens Committee, Inc., supervised the restoration of the buildings and organized the historic collections.

Batsto is reportedly one of the many Pine Barrens communities that regularly receives a visit from the Jersey Devil, the horned, winged monster who has been seen flying through the skies over South Jersey for more than 250 years. Other spectral entities also have been sighted in and around the town since it was first settled in the eighteenth century. Joe Mulliner, a highwayman who robbed passing stagecoaches in the 1780s, was said to enjoy making surprise appearances at local dances. After he was captured and hanged, some local residents claimed that his spirit still walked the woods, searching for treasure he had buried there—or at least, a pretty woman who liked to dance.

The Town Today

Listed in both the New Jersey Register of Historic Places and the National Register of Historic Places, Batsto Village is a popular historic site but is also enjoyed by hikers, fishermen, and boaters. The historic buildings are not always open, but visitors can walk the grounds seven days a week. In addition to the owners' mansion, there are about twelve workers' cottages still standing, along with the post office, general store, gristmill, sawmill, and farm buildings. A museum in the visitors center offers interpretation of the site's historic and natural resources.

Also located within the Wharton tract is the Atsion Mansion on Route 206, built in 1826 as a summer house by Samuel Richards, a son of William and Mary Richards. Although nothing remains of the town of Atsion, the visitors center is the site's former general store and the shells of several farm buildings are situated on the property. Down the road are the decaying remains of the Atsion School, a one-room schoolhouse that was used into the early years of the twentieth century.

Directions

Batsto Village is located within Wharton State Forest on Route 542 about seven miles northeast of Hammonton.

CATAWBA

Did the harbor town of Catawba in Atlantic County disappear because of a hex, as many claimed, or were more sinister, earthly reasons involved?

History

By all accounts, Catawba, situated on the east side of the Great Egg Harbor River about four miles south of Mays Landing, should have been a success. After all, it had been planned well, and its residents were hardy, industrious people. But in just a little more than a decade, the small town was abandoned by everyone except an eccentric hermit who showed up one day with no explanation and disappeared just as mysteriously three years after he arrived.

In 1811, George and Amy West of Burlington purchased the first of two parcels of land on which to build a new community. West, a prosperous merchant and a Methodist minister, laid out the town and constructed a mansion so lavish that it was said to rival Joseph Bonaparte's elegant home in Bordentown. The family donated an acre of ground on which they built a wood-frame Methodist church, complete with a tall spire, that they christened Catawba. While the word is Native American for a type of small red grape that grows wild, no one was sure why the Wests chose it for the name of the church and the town that later grew around it.

About twenty families settled in the town after the men were able to find employment in the shipyards in nearby Mays Landing. Life settled into a comfortable routine until May 17, 1826, when the first of many tragedies struck the West family. Thomas Biddle West, fourteen years old, died two days after being taken ill with an unknown illness. Everything returned to normal for the next three years, but then twenty-three-year-old James West died in August 1829 under similar conditions. Two months later, both George and Amy West died just a week apart—once again succumbing to a condition that caused the same symptoms exhibited by both of their sons. At first, local residents wondered if the Wests had contracted a contagious disease from one of the many sailing ships that stopped at their town. Before long, suspicion grew against the oldest remaining son, Joseph, because even though his sisters Charlotte and Marie were still alive, he stood to inherit his father's estate. It was whispered that he had poisoned his brothers and his parents, and Joseph's actions in the weeks that followed did little to appease local doubt. He quickly sealed all the graves, closed the mansion, and simply disappeared one night.

Was Joseph guilty of murder? Area residents later learned that he had made poor investments, which forced him to sell the town and his family home to pay off his debts. Joseph later served a short sentence in jail for forgery, but then disappeared once again from public view. Catawba's new owner, Gen. Enoch Doughty, one of the founders of the Camden & Atlantic Railroad, decided to demolish the West mansion to reuse the lumber for some construction projects in Absecon. By then, residents of the town began to move away in search of jobs and new opportunities. Many of them had begun to believe that their town was hexed.

One night, a grizzled hermit took up residence on the Wests' property. As a lone light was seen flickering around the grounds at night, rumors spread that he was searching for the gold that Joseph West had buried there. Some said that he knew about the gold because he was, in fact, Joseph West himself. Whether or not he ever found what he was looking for, the man disappeared three years later and was never seen again. Reports of the hex, however, lingered well into the twentieth century.

The Town Today

While a handful of riverfront homes and small businesses stand at this location now, nothing is left of the town built by the Wests in the early nineteenth century.

Directions

Catawba is located on CR 559 (Somers Point Road), east of Estell Manor Park. Turn right on West Avenue to Catawba Avenue to enter the town. If you pass Greentree Golf Course on the left, you've gone too far.

ESTELLVILLE

Estellville was once home to a thriving glass factory, which operated in Atlantic County at a time when glass was almost as rare—and as prized—as precious gems.

History

In 1825, John H. Scott established a glassworks at an area in the Pine Barrens known as Stephen's Creek on the Great Egg Harbor River. With the Revolutionary War long over, men like Scott, a property owner from Gloucester County, were interested in developing industry in the newly formed United States of America. Scott planned to make bottles and window glass at his glassworks and hoped to profit from a tariff law passed that same year giving preference to glass made in America. There is no record of whether or not he was successful. It is documented that he sold his factory to Daniel Estell, the scion of a wealthy local family, nine years after he went into business.

Estell was descended from French Huguenots who had fled their homeland in the early eighteenth century to escape religious persecution by the Catholic Church. His ancestors had purchased a large tract of land in West Jersey from King George III of England. Over the years, they continued to amass property until they owned about six thousand acres in the Great Egg Harbor region. Estell had lived in England for a while before following other relatives to America. After he purchased Scott's glassworks, Estell renamed the company and the surrounding community Estellville. At first, he primarily manufactured window glass, which was in great demand as the population of the young country expanded, but competition was fierce and Estell may not have made much of a profit during those early years. In 1840, he received a letter from John Hartman of Philadelphia, offering to rent the glass factory, because Hartman had "some idea of going into the business." Estell apparently answered no, because he continued to run the glassworks. Whether he succeeded by luck or sheer perseverance or a combination of the two, his glass factory grew to include a melting furnace and a cutting house, as well as about fifteen buildings that could accommodate all phases of production. Thirteen workers' homes were situated within walking distance from the job, where the glassblowers spent six days a week from sunup to sundown, turning out different types of ware.

By 1846, Estell's business was also known as the Weymouth Glass Works. The window glass he produced, which enjoyed a good reputation, was distributed under four brands: Greenwood and Extra Greenwood were the premium grades, and Weymouth and Atlantic were the lesser grades. Greenwood, usually made in sheets ranging from 4 x 9 to 24 x 30 inches in size, sold for $5.25 a box. One month, the glasshouse made and sold 473 boxes worth more than $2,000—a substantial sum at a time when the average worker was lucky to bring home ten dollars per week. Agents like Bush & Hillyer of 178 Greenwich Street in Manhattan promoted Estell's products and in return also provided him with raw materials for the glassworks and products for the company store.

Glassblowers during that time were fairly independent and sometimes had to be lured by higher-than-average wages. To find good workers, Estell corresponded regularly with the owners of other glassworks, often accepting itinerant workers. The workers were paid in shinplasters, also known as scrip, that was only good for full value at the company store, a practice that Estell also followed. By the time they paid for their rent, food, and other necessities, there was very little, if anything, left over at the end of the week.

In the second half of the nineteenth century, the glassworks ceased window glass production and focused instead on blowing bottles. With the patent medicine industry on the rise, there was a great demand for colored glass containers. Since most people could not read, the bottles were shaped into different forms that were associated with a specific product. Estell soon employed about eighty men and the village grew to include a gristmill, a sawmill, and a Methodist church. His bottles were shipped to major cities all along the East Coast. With the money flowing in, Estell built a large mansion for himself and his family about two miles from the glassworks, but not everyone apparently enjoyed life in the wilds of South Jersey. The ghost of his wife, Rebecca, who died young, is said to frequent the third floor of the mansion he had built in 1832.

In 1860, Estell sold the glassworks and nineteen acres of ground for $1,500. The buyers may have been Getzinger & Rosenbaum, who operated the works for about fifteen years before it was purchased by Alexander H. Sharp, a lawyer from Salem who wanted to try his luck at glassmaking. Unfortunately, Estellville was by then no match for larger glassworks that were equipped with all the latest technological advances. Sharp was forced to close after two short years in business and the company never opened its doors again.

Despite the glass company's closure, Rebecca reportedly still haunts the mansion where she had spent her short married life. Estellville is also believed by some to be the true home of the Jersey Devil, who reportedly was born there around 1855. New Jersey's official state monster is said to return there every seven years, in addition to haunting Leeds Point, Dorothy, Batsto, and other small rural towns, but he apparently is not alone. In 1905, the *Atlantic City Evening Union* reported, "Estellville has a mystery in a haunted house. Mrs. Bourgeois rented a tenement house to three men. They stayed four days the information here is that their nerves couldn't hold out no longer against the unearthly sounds and rapping at the door about 3 o'clock each morning."

The Town Today

The remains of Estellville Glassworks and the Estell family home, listed in both the New Jersey Register of Historic Places and the National Register of Historic Places, are now part of the Estell Manor branch of the Atlantic County Parks system. In 1993, Atlantic County purchased the Estell mansion, which had been home to Estell's granddaughter, Rebecca Estell Bourgeois Winston. Winston, who remodeled the house in the 1920s in the Colonial Revival style, was very active in local politics. She persuaded the state legislature to make Estell Manor a municipality in 1924 and was later elected mayor of the town—the first female mayor in New Jersey. Two years later, county officials authorized a stabilization effort to help protect the remains of the melting furnace, the pot house, and other buildings, all that are left of the once-thriving company. To provide easier access for visitors, the park system placed sidewalks and interpretive signs around the ruins of the glassworks.

Directions

Take Route 40 east into Mays Landing. At the intersection of Route 40 and Route 50, turn right on Route 50. Stay on Route 50 for about two miles, and then look for the entrance to the Atlantic County Park on the left. The remains of the glass works are located behind the visitors center.

SCULLVILLE

The tiny town of Scullville in Atlantic County is today a place most people pass through without a second glance on their way to the shore.

History

John and Judiah Jeffryes were among the first European immigrants to move to the heavily wooded, isolated region along the Great Egg Harbor River that would eventually be named in honor of their family. They built an elegant two-story plantation house on the river where they raised their three sons and the settlement soon became known as Jeffries Landing. John Sr. died in 1810, but at a town meeting held on March 10, 1819, John Jr. was named as the wharf master for the town. It was his job to keep track of all the ships and the cargo that went in and out of the port. Ships were charged thirty cents a day once they finished loading or unloading their cargo. The money was used to keep the wharfs repaired and pay the wharf master's salary. After the rates were raised to fifty cents a day by 1827, the wharfs eventually fell into disrepair and were torn down. But even after they were gone, local residents still shipped produce and cordwood from the site.

All of the Jeffryes' sons intermarried with other local families, including the Smiths. Although Jeffries Landing remained the town's name for many years, it was in 1885 listed as Jeffers on the U.S. Geological Survey topographic map of New Jersey. Later, the community was christened Scullville in honor of another family who settled there in the late seventeenth century.

William Lake, one of the founders of nearby Ocean City who died around 1716, left about 450 acres on the Great Egg Harbor River to his son Nathan. After his marriage to Mary Scull, the daughter of Peter Scull, who had arrived in the region in 1695, Nathan sold about 200 acres to Return and Abigail (Cressee) Badcock. Other descendants of the Scull clan included Joseph Scull, who moved to the town before 1870. Joseph, who married Hannah Parvin Gifford of English

Creek, ran a general store in the front of his house and served as the town's postmaster. After he died, Elisha T. Lee took over as the store-keeper. Lee's daughter Ethel inherited the store from him and ran it until 1962.

Before 1805, local residents built the Union Meeting House on the road leading from English Creek to Mays Landing. The meetinghouse was used by the Protestant faction of the Methodist church in the 1830s and later by the congregation of the Asbury Methodist Episcopal Church after their church burned. In 1866, a Methodist Protestant Church was erected in Scullville.

During the War of 1812, John R. Scull gathered his friends and neighbors into a militia to protect their portion of the coast. They built a fort about twenty feet wide and fifteen feet high along the inlet at Somers Point and mounted six cannon along the top. Dubbed the Sand Fort, because it was situated at the water's edge, eight companies of infantry as well as two companies of cavalry were stationed there. Sentries stood guard around the clock and were ordered to fire two shots to alert their neighbors if they observed any enemy approaching. Tunnels, which were destroyed in the late nineteenth century during a construction boom, were dug beneath the fort to store powder.

After the war, a number of homes were built in Scullville to accommodate an influx of new residents. They included a small, one-story house built around 1827 by Isaac and Dolly Jackson, one of twelve African-American families who lived in Egg Harbor Township at that time. The house was later bought by Israel Steelman, who enlarged it into a two-story structure with an addition at the back for cooking. By around 1835, some of the population found work at Thomas Bevis's Carding Mill, which opened on a branch of Lakes Creek. The one-story building with a loft was about forty feet by twenty feet in size. There, wool from local sheep was carded and prepared for market, a job that had once been performed at home. For about eight cents a pound, the carding machine produced combed wool that was drawn through a funnel into a ribbonlike strand. The wool was later returned to the individual farmers in rolls ready to be spun. Bevis's mill closed in 1865 and the machinery was later transported by sailing ship to New York.

Like most small towns, Scullville had a one-room school that was replaced around 1860 by a four-room building that included a stage for entertainment. At the time, male teachers were paid about $33 a month while unmarried women received $20 a month. Since there was no janitor, the boys were responsible for tending the fire, sweeping the building, and bringing in water from the pumphouse. In 1915, the town built a brick school that still stands today.

Some shipbuilding apparently went on in Scullville in the late nineteenth century. The twenty-five-foot sloop *Sally Mason*, which later made its home in neighboring Somers Point, was built there in 1894. The town became a popular resort at about that same time. Visitors stayed at the Hollingsworths' boardinghouse and enjoyed bathing, fishing, and boating on the river. In keeping with the fashion of the day, the town even built a bathhouse for the convenience of the bathers, but it was later washed away in the tide.

Life in the tiny coastal community was not always peaceful, however. In 1907, an arsonist burned down the sawmill that belonged to M. V. B. Scull. Authorities believed that the blaze may have been started by the same person responsible for setting fires in the surrounding forest. Local newspapers reported in 1912 that Mrs. Wesley Somers accidentally shot and killed her nineteen-year-old son Boice with a handgun he had just finished cleaning. The incident generated such sympathy for Mrs. Somers that no further investigation was made by the police. According to the *Atlantic City Evening Union*, the consensus was that she had been "sufficiently punished."

Twelve years later, local residents were shocked by the actions of David Gephart, a forty-eight-year-old farmer and fish dealer who had assaulted his wife, children, and grandchildren. Local papers reported that Gephart violently shook his seven-year-old grandson, who had been crying, and then attacked first his daughter and then his son when they tried to intervene. After Gephart kicked his wife when she got involved, the children ran out of the house in search of help. Gephart, who was arrested the following day by Constable Jesse

Woodington, was charged with assault and battery and attempt to kill. He was held on $3,000 bail while he awaited trial.

The Town Today

Scullville is currently home to the Patcong Marina, a popular stop for those who enjoy boating and fishing. There are a number of historic homes still standing in the town, although many of them are sadly neglected. Among them is the Beaston-Winner House, a two-story frame house built in 1818 on thirty-two acres, purchased by John and Submittee Beaston for $340 from David and Elizabeth Somers.

Directions

Scullville is located on the mainland, southeast of English Creek and northwest of Ocean City on Route 559. If you reach Somers Point, you've gone too far.

BROTHERTON

When European immigrants began flooding into the New World, the Lenni Lenape hoped to find sanctuary at Brotherton, the first Indian reservation in America. It was established in the mid-eighteenth century in the heart of Burlington County.

History

The Lenni Lenape, or "original people," as they called themselves, were primarily peaceful—hunting, fishing, and farming the land that would later become known as New Jersey. While the tribes were divided into the Unami in the central region, the Unilatchtigo in the south, and the Munsee in the north, they roamed freely from place to place, trading with each other and enjoying the bounty that surrounded them. By the eighteenth century, however, the ever-increasing flow of immigrants from different countries in Europe forced the Native Americans to fight for their rights or flee westward. Many chose to fight, and the newly formed colonial government became concerned over the rising death toll among the colonists.

Realizing that they had to create some type of compromise, New Jersey governor Francis Bernard and other officials of the colony met with Teedyuscung, the tribal chieftain, in 1758 to discuss a treaty. Under its terms, the colonists would provide the Indians with a tract of land in Burlington County for their exclusive use. Known by the Lenni Lenape as Edgepillock, or the "place of pure clear water," the site of roughly three thousand acres would later be renamed Brotherton, the first Indian reservation. Ironically, the name was supposed to reflect the spirit of brotherhood between the Native Americans and the colonists. The governor later wrote to the Lords of Trade, informing them that the town had been well organized for the new residents and that he hoped if "I can but keep them from being supplied with rum, for which there are laws strict enough, I shall hope to make them orderly & useful Subjects."

In March 1759, Rev. John Brainerd, a Presbyterian minister from Scotland, was chosen by government officials to serve as the supervisor of Brotherton. In addition to his duties there, Brainerd was a trustee at the College of New Jersey at Princeton and preached at local churches. He often covered a grueling number of miles each week on horseback to handle all of his responsibilities. He had been promised sufficient financial support for "his Indians," but the minister soon discovered that officials were not interested in helping the Native Americans once they had moved onto the site. While some aid was supplied by the Presbyterian Synod and the College of New Jersey, Brainerd was distressed over the government's failure to provide for the tribe. Although the reported number of Indians who moved onto the reservation ranges from four hundred to roughly five thousand, it quickly became apparent that they would have to fend for themselves. Only ten wooden houses built in traditional European style were ready for the Lenni Lenape when they arrived. Brainerd spent $200 of his own money to build a log church at Brotherton and was never reimbursed. He soon found himself selling off his own possessions in order to make ends meet.

According to the minister's journals, Brainerd tried unsuccessfully to get the Lenni Lenape interested in new techniques of farming and other means of making a living. A sawmill had been built at the reservation, but few of them were interested in learning the trade. Some found employment at nearby iron foundries or glassworks, but most were too demoralized to work. Even though they were technically free to leave, the Native Americans remained at Brotherton, and over time, alcohol and disease began to decimate the population.

By 1765, very few residents still lived there. To them, it was not an honorable way of life—it lacked the dignity they had enjoyed in the days before the Europeans had arrived on their shores. That spring, they were invited to join other Lenni Lenape who had moved to the Ohio territory after the French and Indian War, but the Indians living at Brotherton chose to stay in New Jersey at that time, waiting for the outcome of discussions about their future between their representatives and the colonial government. After Brainerd left in 1774, Brotherton was without leadership. When John Hunt, a Quaker preacher from Moorestown, visited the reservation in January 1777, he reportedly found the Indians "in very low circumstances."

In 1801, the Brotherton band received another invitation, this time from the Mahicans (also known as the Stockbridge Indians) who lived near Oneida Lake in New York. The Lenni Lenape asked the colonial government to sell the reservation so they could use the proceeds to move north, but another year passed before all the necessary signatures were obtained. When the caravan finally headed north, only about two hundred Indians made the journey; it was a far cry from the number who had arrived at Brotherton all those years before. The tribe stayed in New York for a short time, but then decided to move west to Green Bay, Wisconsin. In the meantime, Brotherton had been divided into parcels. In March 1802, the state legislature ran an ad in the *Trenton Federalist* offering one hundred-acre plots for sale. Twenty-five different colonists bought the ground for prices ranging from $2 to $5 per acre.

Almost fifty years after it was opened as a commitment to brotherhood, the state officially closed America's first Indian reservation.

The Indians never received any money from that sale. Thirty years later, Bartholomew S. Calvin, a member of the tribe who had been educated at Princeton and who had fought in the Revolutionary War, approached the New Jersey State Legislature and asked that the Lenni Lenape be awarded a $2,000 settlement for the property at Brotherton to finally cancel out that long-standing debt. The legislators apparently agreed and ordered the state treasurer to make payment in full.

While the majority of the tribe had moved on, the best-known descendant of the Native Americans who lived at Brotherton was Ann Ashatama, born about 1805 on the John Woolman farm near Rancocas Creek. Better known by the locals as Indian Ann, she was the daughter of Elisha Ashatama, a Lenni Lenape who had lived at Brotherton, and an unknown mother. Ashatama had gone north with the remainder of the tribe in 1802, but returned shortly afterward to New Jersey and moved into a cabin on the Woolman farm. Ann first married Peter Green, a former slave, but little is known about their life together. Her second husband was John Roberts from Virginia, with whom she had seven children. They lived in a small frame house on Dingletown Road. Roberts died on July 15, 1852, in the Burlington County Almshouse in New Lisbon. Ann later applied for and received a pension from the government because her son, John Roberts Jr., had served in Company A, 22nd Regiment of Colored Troops of the Union Army, during the Civil War. Ann declared that she had the right to claim the money because John Jr., as her youngest child, had been her only means of support. John Jr. had died in a hospital in Yorktown, Virginia, after serving thirteen months in the military.

Ann received a pension of $8 a month, which increased to $12 when she was eighty-two. She remained at the family homestead until she died, weaving baskets, as she had been taught by her father, that are prized today by collectors. Buried in an unmarked grave in the Tabernacle Cemetery near her home, Ann's site was later marked by the Tabernacle Historical Society. In addition, the Indian Mills Historical Society has placed a roadside marker beneath the pines near the location of her former home that reads as follows: "Indian Ann,

Celebrated Ann Roberts, last of the Delawares in the State, resided here until her death in 1894. She has become a legend in the Pines."

The Town Today

Nothing remains of the settlement at Brotherton, other than a historical marker outlining the events that occurred there. The residents of the neighboring town of Indian Mills, settled in 1876, have worked hard to preserve a number of Colonial- and Victorian-era homes that reflect those early days of settlement.

Directions

Take Route 206 north through Hammonton past the Atsion Recreation Area. Turn left on Forked Neck Road (CR 620) into Indian Mills. Brotherton was located just northwest of the town on Indian Mills Sawmill Pond.

CHAIRVILLE

Like Brotherton, a historical marker is the only indication of the location where the village of Chairville once stood in Burlington County.

History

The early settlers to New Jersey sometimes adopted whimsical names for their new hometowns, while others opted for a variation on the Native American tongue. Sometimes, though, the less imaginative would pick a certain feature to describe their new community, as in the case of Chairville. The town was christened accordingly because it was home to a chair parts factory, which operated there between 1845 and the 1880s. A sawmill, known as Peacock's Mill or the Steam Turning Mill, which started at about the same time, remained in business for about another ten years after the chair factory went out of business. The town consisted of about six houses, a grocery store, and a one-room schoolhouse that served local children until the turn of the twentieth century.

Although it might sound like just another mundane town, life was not always quiet and peaceful in the little community. According to the *New Jersey Mirror*, Chairville was the site of a brutal murder in 1907. On April 27 of that year, a "gang of hoodlums" from the neighboring town of Tabernacle decided to get drunk and crash a dance at the home of Irwin Mathis. They arrived a little past midnight and began to cause trouble but were confronted by David Beebe, a forty-two-year-old farmer who lived on the road between Red Lion and Medford. Beebe, married with five children, had decided to stop in at the dance while on his way home from Medford that night. He ordered the troublemakers to depart, but they, in turn, warned him to mind his own business or suffer the consequences. Described by the newspaper as "a tall man of unusual physical development," Beebe disregarded the threat and bravely took on the entire group. Then, one of the intruders knocked Beebe down with a club and the thugs ultimately beat him to death.

Mathis, in the meantime, had sped off to find the local constable, but by the time he returned shortly after two o'clock in the morning, Beebe's lifeless body was lying in the road. Sheriff Norcross and his deputy, Joseph Fleetwood, soon arrested Howard Reeves, Harvey Reeves, Theodore Wells, Caleb Rogers, and Harry Hammell for murder and transported them to the Mount Holly Jail. The following day, Charles Spicker of Chairville and Walter "Baldy" Simons of Red Lion were also arrested and charged with the crime. A witness, Howard Beebe, who was Beebe's nephew, told authorities that Rogers hit his uncle at least four times during the assault.

Coroner Seeds performed an autopsy and determined that Beebe, who had been healthy, had died of a concussion as the result of being struck with a blunt object. An inquest was held in Medford on May 8 and a huge crowd listened spellbound as witnesses related the events of that fatal night. Clifford D. Prickitt stated that he saw Rogers kick Beebe "about the body" after knocking him down. Rogers then jumped on Beebe's stomach with both knees, seized him by the throat, and pounded him on the head. Simons, he stated, then took a hand in the attack and gave Beebe several kicks. Following the inquest, officers brought Rogers, Wells, Simons, and Harvey Reeves back to the Mount Holly Jail. Howard Reeves, Harry Hammell, and Charles Spicker were discharged immediately after the inquest.

Indicted for manslaughter by a special session of the grand jury, Caleb Rogers, Theodore Wells, and Walter Simons were brought to trial on September 11, 1907, but scheduling conflicts for the attorneys caused the trial to be delayed several times before the case was heard. On November 20, the newspaper reported that after a twenty-hour session, the jury returned the following verdicts: Caleb Rogers, found guilty, was sentenced to the Rahway Reformatory, while Theodore Wells, convicted of atrocious assault, was sentenced to three months in the county jail and to pay a $200 fine. Simons was acquitted by the court.

The Town Today

Don't bother trying to find Chairville now. All that's left is a roadside historical marker just outside of Medford noting the town's location at the intersection of Route 70 and Chairville Road. Nothing remains of the town that once manufactured chair parts except for the name, which appears on a street sign and a local elementary school.

Directions

Take Route 206 north to Route 70 west, until it intersects with Chairville Road on the left.

CHATSWORTH

Both American and European aristocracy once vacationed in the remote town of Chatsworth in Burlington County.

History

Tucked northeast of the historic site of Batsto Village, the town of Chatsworth was designated in 1967 as "The Capital of the Pine Barrens" by author John McPhee, who wrote several books about New

Jersey history. Many of the more than eight hundred residents of the tiny community have roots there that are as deep as some of the trees in the surrounding forest. For the most part, they live on First, Second, and Third Streets, some in homes that date back to Chatsworth's earliest years of settlement when it was known simply as Shamong.

In 1800, the twenty-five-thousand-acre tract that included Chatsworth was known as the J. D. Beers tract. Beers, a New York realty tycoon, left a fortune to his heirs, who later established the Chatsworth Park Company. One of the town's oldest landmarks is the White Horse Inn, originally called the Shamong Hotel, which was built as a stagecoach stop in the early nineteenth century. When the Central Railroad of New Jersey constructed a line past the town, passengers from New York and Philadelphia stopped there briefly before traveling on to the Chatsworth Country Club. The cedar-sided inn, with eleven fireplaces, remained in business as a boardinghouse for many years afterward before it was abandoned.

Like many Pinelands communities, Chatsworth suffered when the iron and glass industries collapsed in the mid-nineteenth century. Many longtime residents moved away in search of work. By the late 1800s, newcomers like Willis Jefferson Buzby moved into town; he purchased the general store, which remained a family-owned business for almost fifty years. Like most general stores, it was a central location for residents to meet and exchange local news as well as shop for goods such as food, hunting supplies, sewing needs, and farm equipment. After Buzby died, his son Jack operated the store until his death. The owners that later ran the store were apparently not as capable businessmen, however, because it was eventually sold for unpaid taxes.

Like many Burlington County towns, Chatsworth depended heavily on cranberry production to ensure its survival. While the residents worked hard to make a living, the town was also home to an exclusive private club whose blue-blooded members enjoyed the finest that money could buy. The club had been started by Prince Mario Ruspoli de Poggio-Suasa, an attaché to the Italian embassy in Washington, who had married Palma de Talleyrand Perigold, the granddaughter of J. D. Beers. Palma's dowry included seven thousand acres of Pinelands with cranberry bogs. Around 1900, the prince built a luxurious Queen Anne-style villa near town, modeled after Chatsworth, the English country home of the Duke of Devonshire. To reinforce the idea of a country house surrounded by a village, he persuaded local officials to change the name of Shamong to Chatsworth.

The prince built a lavish country club on the grounds of his estate as a retreat for his wealthy friends and business associates who soon formed the Chatsworth Park Company and purchased the property from him. Before long, about seven hundred members regularly visited the Chatsworth Club, including the Vanderbilts, Astors, J. P. Morgan, Jay Gould, and Vice President Levi Morton. The nation's elite considered the lakefront Chatsworth Club, with its stables, golf courses, and landscaped trails, to be the equal of Newport, Rhode Island, then one of the country's most prestigious vacation spots where the "cottages" of millionaires stood along the coast. In 1907, however, the Trust Company of America foreclosed on the property. In November of that year, Sheriff Norcross was ordered by the court in Mount Holly to hold an auction for the more than five thousand acres owned by the Chatsworth Park Company.

Abandoned in the years that followed, the Chatsworth Club met its end in the 1930s, when a spark from the Blue Comet, a specialty train, touched off a raging fire. The Blue Comet had previously brought many members to town, making daily runs from Jersey City in less than three hours through the Pine Barrens to Hammonton and Atlantic City. Owned and operated by the Central Railroad of New Jersey, everything on the high-speed train was blue, from the tickets to the seats to the diesel engine. Some local residents say that if you listen carefully on a warm summer night, you just might hear the sound of a train whistle blowing close by. That might not be uncommon except that the tracks going by the town have been rusted out and unused for about eighty years. The Blue Comet made its last run on the night of August 19, 1939, when a washed-out section of tracks just outside of Chatsworth sent it flying off the rails, killing hundreds.

The Town Today

About two hundred homes still stood in Chatsworth in 1999. At that time, the Chatsworth Cranberry Company, formed almost a century ago, was the state's second-largest producer of cranberries. Eight years later, *National Geographic Adventure* magazine dubbed the community one of America's best small towns, because of the thriving ecosystem that surrounded Chatsworth. New owners restored Buzby's General Store in the 1990s and preserved many of its original features. The fireplace dates from 1865 and still bears the footprints of the raccoons who walked across the bricks before they had completely dried. Listed in the National Register of Historic Places, the general store's outhouse has been the site of many archaeological digs. Efforts to restore the White Horse Inn have been progressing slowly, but the new owners of that building hope that they will also be able to restore it to its original condition someday. Chatsworth annually hosts a cranberry festival in October and the funds that are raised are used to support the project.

Directions

The tiny community of Chatsworth sits at the intersection of Route 532 and Route 563, deep in the heart of the Pine Barrens.

ONG'S HAT

For generations, New Jersey residents have puzzled over the mystery of who was Ong and how did his hat wind up in a tree in the wilds of Burlington County?

History

Hidden within the confines of Brendan T. Byrne State Forest lies a network of ghost towns, each of which has its own tale to tell. None of them, however, bear a name as unique as Ong's Hat, believed to have been founded in the early nineteenth century. There are different versions of how the town acquired its unusual name.

Although the Swedish surname Ong was common among early settlers in the region, it eventually died out when the family moved away. Some say the "hat" belonged to Jacob Ong, a Swede who frequented the region until about 1835. Ong apparently loved to dance and have a good time, but one night, a woman reportedly snatched his hat from his head and stomped on it in a jealous rage because he wasn't paying enough attention to her. In frustration, Ong tossed the flattened hat in the air, where it caught on the high branch of a pine tree. Another story claims it was a different Ong, who in a drunken fit threw his top hat high into the branches of a pine tree where it remained for many years. This Ong was also said to be a fixture at local dances, where his tall silk hat and his charm impressed the women. Another more mundane version claims that Ong was a tavern keeper who simply painted a silk hat on the sign outside his door to attract customers to his classy establishment.

An Ong family descendant debunked those tales in a letter published in 1968 in the *New York Times*. According to him, the Ongs lived in Little Egg Harbor in the early seventeenth century and had their grain ground at a mill in Burlington County. Since transporting the grain was such an arduous journey, they built a hut where they could rest overnight. This way station, known simply as Ong's Hut, was later transformed into the more colorful Ong's Hat. Regardless of how the name came into use, Ong's Hat was often described as just a handful of houses and a dancehall, which drew revelers each week from throughout the county for the music, bare-knuckle boxing in an outdoor ring, and homemade white lightning that flowed freely from local stills.

Like many small towns in the region, Ong's Hat fell on hard times as industry left the area. In the 1890s, a local resident named Samuel Harris was arrested for selling liquor without a license. A few years later, John Chininiski and his wife, immigrants from Poland, moved there, but by that point only seven people lived in the town. Very little was known about the couple, despite the questions that were raised when Chininiski's wife disappeared. As rumors spread, he vanished as well, leaving their house and their few belongings behind.

Chininiski reportedly had fled to New York, but his whereabouts were never discovered. Most of the remaining residents of Ong's Hat packed up and left some years later after a hunting party came upon a woman's skeleton in the surrounding woods—believed to be the remains of Mrs. Chininiski. Burlington County sheriff Ellis Parker reportedly kept the skull in his office for many years as a reminder of the unsolved case.

By 1936, Eli Freed, a seventy-nine-year-old farmer originally from Chicago, was the last remaining resident of Ong's Hat. Most of the homes there had disintegrated with age, leaving behind just a few foundations or piles of rubble as evidence they had ever existed.

The Town Today

Nothing much more than the name, which still appears on some maps, and a few foundations overgrown by the forest mark the place where Ong's Hat once stood.

The town might have eventually settled into obscurity except that its name and location were co-opted in recent years by Joseph Matheny for a book titled *Ong's Hat: The Beginning*, which recounts tales from websites about a cult of outcast scientists who allegedly opened an interdimensional gateway in Ong's Hat to travel to different worlds.

Directions

Ong's Hat is located on New Jersey Route 72, west of the intersection with Route 70.

PASADENA

Starting a clay factory in the midst of the forest in Burlington County seemed like a good idea at the time, but tragedy struck Pasadena before work even began, leaving the proposed company town in ruins.

History

If you're thinking you took a wrong turn somewhere and wound up in California, guess again. Once upon a time, there really was a Pasadena, New Jersey. Although it's now not much more than some broken bits of a vine-covered building and a name on a map, Pasadena was going to be home to South Jersey's first major clay factory. In 1866, a businessman named Daniel Townsend, a successful war profiteer, decided to open the Townsend Clay Manufacturing Company in a section of Manchester Township known as Wheatland. Business boomed when the Raritan & Delaware Bay Railroad laid its tracks close by the factory and local bankers decided they wanted to invest in Townsend's company. In 1873, Townsend and his new partners incorporated the Wheatland Manufacturing Company, which operated until Townsend died in 1878.

Five years after Townsend's death, his partners decided they would rather develop real estate than manufacture clay articles. They drew up plans for a new town on the site of the factory, christened it Pasadena, and initially sold a number of lots. Despite the initial interest, however, no one ever moved to Pasadena. By 1915, not a single house had been built. At almost the same time, the Brooksbrae Brick Company was built on about five thousand acres just south of the proposed development to manufacture bricks for the Adams Clay Mining Company. Although the state-of-the-art plant has been mistakenly identified over the years as the Pasadena Terra Cotta Company, Brooksbrae, which cost more than $10,000 to build, was intended to produce thousands of bricks per day. After the company owner, William J. Kelly, died in 1908, litigation over his estate apparently kept the plant from going into operation.

There are several stories about raging fires that later kept Brooksbrae from ever opening. In 1915, workers from the Central Railroad of New Jersey reportedly staged a strike at Brooksbrae, shutting down the trains in that area. As tensions continued to flare, the brick company's owners sent Jonas Tomaszewski and his wife out to protect the site. When the elderly caretakers lit a fire in their stove one cold night, the clogged flue forced smoke into the house where they slept. Before long, a fire roared out of control. While local authorities determined that no foul play had been involved, a story spread that the fire had been set to cover up the couple's murder.

Another tragedy, reported in the local newspapers the following year, stated that Samuel Chattin, who lived with his family in the area, saw smoke roiling out of the plant around noon. When he and his son rushed to the plant, they peered in a window to see the body of Chattin's twelve-year-old daughter, Hannah, lying prone on a cot next to Gildo Plazziano, an Austrian immigrant who was then acting as the watchman there. They both had apparently been overcome by the smoke, but curiously enough, Plazziano's arms, legs, and head were missing when he was later pulled from the room. The watchman, who made no secret of his interest in Hannah, was described as a loner by local residents. Local officials, after discovering candy and other gifts for the child in Plazziano's room, determined that he had raped and then murdered her before setting fire to the plant to hide his crime.

Three years after the murder, the dispute over William Kelly's will was finally settled and the executors were able to sell the Brooksbrae factory. Unfortunately, the multiple tragedies that had occurred there apparently discouraged anyone from opening the plant.

The Town Today

Later renamed Wheatlands, the overgrown remains of Pasadena and the Brooksbrae factory are unprotected from vandals or the elements and are a favorite playground for paintballers.

Directions

From the Route 70/Route 72 circle, take Route 70 east to Route 539. Make a right onto Route 539 south to McMahon Avenue. Turn right and watch for Buckingham Road on your right, as well as some old railroad tracks. About a mile past Buckingham Road, look for trees marked with white patches. Pull over and walk into the woods at this point. In about five minutes, you will reach Pasadena.

TIMBUCTOO

In recent years, archaeologists have started to uncover the lives as well as the homes of the African Americans who settled in the small Burlington County town called Timbuctoo.

History

Some local residents still recall the aging Victorian homes that stood in the tiny town of Timbuctoo as late as the 1950s. Commonly called Bucto, the settlement along the Rancocas Creek in Westampton Township was founded around 1820 by free blacks and former slaves with the support of local Quakers like John Woolman and Samuel Aaron. The African-American settlement near Mount Holly may have been named after the famed city that flourished as a cultural center in West Africa between the fourteenth and sixteenth centuries. By the mid-nineteenth century, more than 125 people lived in New Jersey's Timbuctoo. The town, which appeared on Burlington County maps as early as 1849, was also home to a school, an African Methodist Episcopal Zion Church, and a hotel built in 1855 by carpenter Jacob Dufford.

With their own memories of slavery sometimes still vividly painful, the residents of Timbuctoo quickly turned their town into a way station on the Underground Railroad. They often drove off slave catchers who wanted to capture the fugitives who had found sanctuary there. Otherwise, they married, raised their children, and buried their dead, including popular residents like Hezekiah Hall, who was laid to rest on February 21, 1851, at the age of about sixty. Hall, respected and mourned by the community, had been a slave belonging to Charles Carroll of Carrollton, Georgia, but escaped in 1814.

On February 13, 1862, the *New Jersey Mirror* reported that Perry Simmons, a fugitive slave who had repeatedly escaped capture thanks to his watchful neighbors, had died in Timbuctoo a week earlier. The paper stated that Simmons had suffered a severe cold after the most recent effort by slave catchers to return him to the South. Simmons, who "was forced to fly suddenly from his bedroom to the garret, where he was obliged to remain till morning," never recuperated from his cold and was finally "beyond the reach of his Southern masters."

Like the residents of other small communities, some families in Timbuctoo suffered financial setbacks. On November 13, 1867, Martha Harker's property was seized and sold at public auction. The four-and-a-half acre tract was heavily forested with pine that was suitable as cordwood. But for every setback, there were happy occasions like the wedding of John Sanders and an unknown bride on October 14, 1868. The affair was held at Sanders's home with no cards "but lots of home-made gingerbread." The newlyweds planned to honeymoon at Mineral Spring.

In 1880, the U.S. census determined that 108 residents lived in twenty-nine households in Timbuctoo. The population remained roughly the same in the years that followed—if no one counted some of the alleged spectral residents. In February 1929, the *New York Times* reported that three ghosts, two white and one black, had appeared there at the home of Walter Treichler. The retired chemist claimed that he had been awakened shortly after midnight by the sound of mysterious tapping, footsteps, and moaning. Although a medium and some police detectives investigated the incident, they could find no cause, either natural or supernatural, for the occurrence at the Treichler house. While some suspected that the intruders may have been members of the Ku Klux Klan, local residents were still talking about the haunting ten years later. Others placed more belief in the occult powers of the woman who lived in the "Witch House." They reportedly passed her home quickly, especially at night.

The Town Today

A geological survey conducted in recent years showed evidence that much of the town's history, including as many as eighteen houses and Timbuctoo's first church, lie underground. In 2010, archaeologists from Temple University in Philadelphia began to excavate a hill next to the cemetery where a house once stood. Their discoveries included broken pieces of dinner plates, a silver clasp from a woman's handbag, and piles of mason jars, buried among the foundations.

Interest in the excavation has also focused new attention on the small cemetery located next to the site. In 2010, the cemetery was officially designated as the Timbuctoo Civil War Memorial Cemetery, in recognition of the African-American veterans who had served in the Union Army. Over the years, the Westhampton American Legion Post 509 has helped maintain the graves of twelve soldiers who are buried there, including Louis B. Armstrong, Charles Love, and Edward Chapman, who served in the Army's 22nd Regiment, and William W. Sullivan, who served in the 29th Regiment.

Directions

Timbuctoo is located on Rancocas Road just west of the Mount Holly city limits and just east of Rancocas State Park and Route 295.

WHITESBOG

Today, millions of Americans know that the tiny blueberry has important nutritional value, but not everyone is familiar with the fact that it was first cultivated for mass consumption in the rural Burlington County community of Whitesbog.

History

Although Whitesbog's history is more closely tied to the blueberry, its story actually began with another fruit, the cranberry, which grew wild in the swampy bogs of the great forest known as the New Jersey Pine Barrens. That property that was originally home to the Hanover Iron Furnace was bought by Col. James A. Fenwick and became a town in the mid-nineteenth century. Fenwick began cultivating the plentiful supply of tangy red berries that quickly became a household favorite. By the 1860s, Fenwick's bogs were annually producing about fifty barrels of cranberries that sold for about $10 apiece in America and $20 each in Europe.

Fenwick's granddaughter, Elizabeth White, was raised at Whitesbog. At a young age, she became interested in cultivating the wild blueberries that grew around the cranberry bogs. Since the blueberries ripened each July, and the cranberries weren't ready for harvesting until September, she realized the town could produce two annual crops instead of one. Unfortunately, most of the local farmers were skeptical of cultivating blueberries; they believed the plants were too wild to tame. Additionally, White had no agricultural training or education, so no one believed that her efforts would meet with success. But in 1911, White contacted Dr. Frederick V. Coville, who had worked in the field of blueberry cultivation. She convinced her father that the doctor's work deserved their support and persuaded Coville to move to Whitesbog to continue his research.

While the doctor studied different methods of propagating the fruit, White gathered local residents and asked them to search the forests for the best blueberry bushes they could find. Using Coville's methods of hybridization, Whitesbog produced its first batch of cultivated blueberries in 1916. In a few years, the town was home to ninety acres of bushes that were harvested each summer. In 1927, White helped organize the New Jersey Blueberry Cooperative Association and became the first female member of the American Cranberry Association. She received a citation for her work from the New Jersey Department of Agriculture. Respected as a major producer of blueberries, White remained at her home at Whitesbog, Suningive, until her death in 1954.

The Town Today

The community remains fairly intact thanks to the efforts of the Whitesbog Preservation Association. Formed in 1982, the organization is headquartered at Suningive, which is currently open to the public as a museum. In addition to the general store, farm buildings, and cottages, visitors can see several bungalows in town that were mail-order purchases from Sears in the early 1900s. Sold for about $2,000 at that time, the houses arrived in sections and were advertised as being easily assembled in ninety days. Some are still private residences, so be careful not to trespass.

Directions

From the New Jersey Turnpike, take Exit 7 to Route 206 south to the intersection of Route 206, Route 38, and Route 530. Turn east onto Route 530 and follow it to Mile Marker 13.

ANCORA

For many people, Ancora's history has been long overshadowed by the scandals at its notorious psychiatric hospital. Yet there is a lot more to this Camden County town, including the story of a group of social reformers who simply wanted to live off the land.

History

During the eighteenth and nineteenth centuries, it was common for European immigrants to buy thousands of acres of ground in West Jersey, where their families established strong roots that endure into the twenty-first century. The area that would eventually be known as Ancora was no exception. The Albertsons were among the earliest settlers in the region. Around 1826, twenty-seven-year-old David Albertson is believed to have built the Spring Garden Inn near Blew (later Blue) Anchor. The two-and-a-half story, eighteen-room, stone-and-timber structure with brick chimneys was originally known as The Sign of the Sorrel Horse, but was renamed the Spring Garden Inn soon afterward. It was located on a major roadway about seventy miles from Cape May, which was an important vacation spot at the time.

Built at the east corner of the intersection of the White Horse Pike and Spring Road, the inn was located just three miles east of the Blew Anchor Tavern, which was owned and operated by David's parents, Josiah and Ann Albertson. Both taverns were built on the 750 acres that Josiah had purchased for $4,000 from the estate of his father-in-law Robert Mattocks. The Albertson family continued to spread its roots throughout the region and the Spring Garden Inn remained in their possession for generations. In the 1940s, it was restored by the Beebes, Albertson descendents, and later listed in the New Jersey Register of Historic Places.

Longtime residents like the Albertsons were probably either scandalized or amused during the late nineteenth and early twentieth centuries, when a number of individuals and groups established utopian colonies in New Jersey. While they were often guided by different philosophies, the groups all seemed to agree that farming and communal living were the only antidotes to life in the city, which seemed to grow more crowded and dangerous with each passing year. The American Spiritualist movement, which spread rapidly following the Civil War, was well received in many towns throughout New Jersey. In 1871, Ancora was home to a Spiritualist Lyceum, which provided classes and lectures to the public on a variety of subjects. Eben W. Bond was the "conductor," while Emeline E. S. Wood held the post of "guardian." Dr. H. P. Fairfield, who lived in Ancora, was a lecturer there.

The following year, supporters of the Industrial Public movement decided that Ancora would be the perfect spot to start one of their communities. They intended to show the nation that social evolution was possible even under the most difficult conditions. Like other similar groups, they started with good intentions and few skills. Many members of the Ancora Productive Union of the Industrial Public arrived at the colony with nothing more than the clothes on their backs. Unfortunately, they were either extremely poor or had gone bankrupt during a depression that adversely affected both America and Europe's economy. Borrowing tools and equipment from other local farmers, who patiently showed the newcomers how to work the land, Union members also supported themselves by trying their hands at carpentry, plastering, and other services for their neighbors.

Although they worked hard, early harvests were poor. As a result, some Union members grew discouraged and decided to move back to the cities, where a steady income was offered in exchange for a day's work. As their ranks dwindled, the remaining members finally decided to disband. In their book, *The Industrial Public*, Horace

Fowler and his brother Samuel, who were among the founders of the Ancora colony, later declared, "Although the trial would be called a failure by most people, because finally abandoned, it proved to the satisfaction of the writer and some others that the principles are correct and practical under right conditions."

Despite the fact that the Union collapsed after only three years, another supporter of the utopian movement announced that he was going to start a "free love, Mormon, communistic and socialistic colony at Ancora" in 1881. This time, however, local authorities were not as amenable to the idea and even attempted to prosecute James M. Allen that May at the courthouse in Camden. Allen arrived for his arraignment accompanied by two women who were allegedly his wives. While one of the women wore a scandalous bloomer costume, the other was dressed in a subdued blue suit. Declaring that he would act as his own attorney, Allen soon persuaded the court to dismiss the case on the grounds that he had broken no laws.

Although the freethinkers apparently made no more efforts to settle in Ancora after that, the town thrived thanks in part to the Camden & Atlantic Railroad, which stopped at a station there. In 1883, residents mourned as a wave of smallpox stole the lives of some young residents, while violence and vandalism began to spread. Some blamed the influx of immigrants who were arriving in New Jersey at that time. Area farmers experimented with different fruit crops, but their efforts were not always successful. In 1893, M. M. Walker of Germantown, Pennsylvania, planted peach trees on fifty acres of ground that he owned in Ancora, but the quality was so poor, he only picked three baskets of edible fruit, selling one for $1.00.

In 1900, the town opened its first hospital, but years later, another medical facility would locate there and make the name of Ancora synonymous with the stuff of nightmares. The Ancora Psychiatric Hospital, which opened in 1956 on more than six hundred acres, was originally seen as a facility that offered cutting-edge treatment in the field of mental health. The largest of New Jersey's five public psychiatric hospitals, Ancora even provided workers' housing on the grounds, where doctors, nurses, and other staff lived with their families. But as years passed, the 730-bed hospital, like many similar state agencies, was sabotaged by political corruption and a lack of funding. The quality of care disintegrated, there was overcrowding and neglect, and by the turn of the twenty-first century, horror stories emerged from the facility with frightening regularity.

In July 2006, Salwa Srour, a thirty-six-year-old patient, was arrested by New Jersey State Police for strangling her roommate, fifty-four-year-old Margaret Cetrangolo, in her bedroom. That December, another patient, thirty-five-year-old DeWitt Crandell Jr., hanged himself while he was supposed to be supervised by Ancora staff. Crandell had been admitted to Ancora after stabbing both of his parents to death in 1996. In January 2007, fifty-two-year-old Robert Williams, a patient at Ancora, died at Cooper University Hospital in Camden from abdominal injuries after he was attacked by Tyrell McAllister, twenty-three, during a dispute over a cigarette.

In September of that year, a murderer simply walked away from the hospital grounds and was later discovered hiding out in the nearby forest. Sixty-four-year-old William Enman admitted in 1974 to beating to death his roommate, Peter LeSeur, and the man's four-year-old son, Eric, while living in Morris County. Found not guilty by reason of insanity, Enman was involuntarily committed to other state mental hospitals before being transferred to Ancora in 1992. Over the years, the paranoid schizophrenic has repeatedly asked to be released and made other escape attempts. Despite his record, Enman was permitted to take unsupervised walks around hospital grounds. Such incidents have forced local residents to use extra precaution around their normally quiet town.

While runaway patients may have been a serious problem faced by the residents of Ancora, supernatural entities have also prowled the community from time to time. The Jersey Devil has been periodically sighted over the years, and at different times, the owners of the Spring Garden Inn have reported seeing a blonde woman in a long white dress both inside and outside, while strange noises and voices have been heard in different parts of the building.

The Town Today

The Spring Garden Inn may have been a major stagecoach stop in its day, but there is nothing left of the barns where the horses were once stabled. Fortunately, the inn itself has been well preserved, although in 2011, the owners were seeking to sell.

Suspensions and termination of hospital employees followed each incident at Ancora State Hospital. As of this writing, there were still reports of problems. The hospital was the target of an investigation by the U.S. Department of Justice in 2008, but it remains in operation. Although the workers' housing was torn down by 2004, paranormal investigators claim that the site is host to supernatural activity. One popular urban myth has styled the workers' homes as a "veterans haven," where some of the patients who were veterans of different wars lived. There were reportedly so many murders among the residents there that the village was closed down. Despite the fact that the housing is gone, reports still surface from time to time about spectral sightings there.

Directions

Ancora is located just south of the intersection of Route 143 and Route 30, west of a large section of the Pine Barrens.

WATERFORD WORKS

Waterford Works in Camden County was just one of about two hundred towns that thrived in the 1800s thanks to New Jersey's glassmaking industry.

History

During the nineteenth century, many entrepreneurs looked at the vast forests and network of waterways that wove through South Jersey and decided it was a region ripe for investment. Some had more enthusiasm than ability when it came to business, while others amassed huge fortunes through industries like glassmaking, which had become important even before the Revolutionary War. The southern part of the state was considered ideal for glassmaking, because there was an apparently endless supply of pine trees for fuel and silica sand that was one of the main ingredients.

In 1824, veteran glassblower Jonathan Haines established Waterford Works about twenty miles outside of Philadelphia. Haines, an Irish immigrant, may have named the site for Ireland's famed Waterford glass factory, which produced fine crystal between the late eighteenth and early nineteenth centuries. Haines was a glassblower who in 1804 had run Samuel Clement's glassworks in Clementon. He later moved to Hammonton to work at the company belonging to William Coffin Sr., which produced an assortment of mold-blown flasks in a range of brilliant colors.

After starting Waterford, Haines focused on producing flasks, which were needed by the growing patent medicine industry. Although the glassworks started as a small operation, it soon expanded as demand for its products increased. Unfortunately, Haines died four years after he started Waterford and the business was sold to Thomas Evans, Samuel Shreve, and Jacob Roberts. Joseph Porter, who later acquired an interest in the company, was appointed manager. Under his direction, the glassworks produced window glass, tableware, and hollowware (as bottles were called), which were primarily sold through a sales office in Philadelphia.

Housing for the workers quickly sprang up around the glass factory. Before long, the village boasted a post office, two stores, and churches of different denominations. The Waterford Methodist Episcopal Church was opened in May 1848 on land donated by Porter and Shreve. The two-story frame building was home to the temperance society upstairs, while religious services were held on the ground floor. The congregation of the Waterford Presbyterian Church was formed in April 1866 and they built a frame church with a ninety-foot steeple. The congregation of the Christ Protestant Episcopal Church was organized two years later and the members constructed their church on land donated by William C. Porter.

Joseph Porter, who ultimately acquired a controlling interest in the glassworks, renamed it Joseph Porter & Sons. Around 1863, his son William took control of the glassworks, which by then included two factories, one that produced window panes and another that made bottles. William later sold the entire property to Maurice Raleigh, another investor who owned huge tracts of property in the region. Raleigh made Waterford part of his Atsion estate. In 1880, he built the Waterford Roman Catholic Church for the growing number of Catholic workers who had moved to the region. For a short time, Raleigh took an interest in bottle making and leased the other two glassworks to John Gayner, who made window glass and lamp chimneys. Raleigh apparently was not concerned about modernizing the glassworks, however, so he was unable to keep up with the competition. The buildings soon began to deteriorate and the furnaces were shut down.

To help the townspeople, Raleigh converted one of the glass factories into a hosiery mill, where many residents were employed. He also partnered with James Colter to build a three-story frame shoe factory, where a hundred people worked for about a year. Unfortunately, the shoe business did not make any money, so it was closed and the machinery removed. For a short time afterward, part of the building was used as a shop where textile machinery was repaired, but in May 1882, a fire spread rapidly from that location and destroyed all of the factories. Manufacturing came to an abrupt end as a result, forcing more than half of the local residents to move.

Raleigh's death also affected any chance that Waterford may have had of resuming any manufacturing. His vast estate, run by the Raleigh Land and Improvement Company, was broken into smaller tracts and sold as ideal for agriculture. Investors who decided to try their hand at fruit growing included John W. Hoag, Alexander Heggan, William O. Bisbee, Josiah Albertson, and Godfrey Walker. Some of them decided to farm cranberries, which were stored at Waterford following their harvest.

Josiah Rice opened the first shop in Waterford that was not owned by the glass company. He later sold the store to Lewis Nepling, who built another business on the opposite side of the railroad tracks. Joseph Porter's former home was turned into a hotel around 1858 by a man named Pickett. Dr. Joseph Stout, who lived near Tansboro, was one Waterford's first doctors. Dr. Risley, who also lived near Tansboro, later took over his practice. He was followed by Dr. John Snowden of Spring Garden, then Dr. Joseph North, who lived for a while at Waterford. By the late nineteenth century, Waterford had about 250 residents who still lived in some of the homes constructed during Raleigh's years of ownership.

The Town Today

While Waterford Works has seen some new development in recent years, a number of older homes are still sprinkled throughout the town.

Directions

Waterford Works sits at the intersection of Route 30 and Chew Landing Road, just west Wharton State Forest.

DIAMOND BEACH

The Diamond Beach that most people know today is nothing like the original community in Cape May County that bore that name.

History

Prior to the Civil War, a lot of wealthy Southern families vacationed on the southern edge of New Jersey. Cape May and the surrounding communities were easily accessible by ferry and provided them with all the elegant amenities to which they had become accustomed. The war, however, soon changed all that, and afterward, the hotels and boardinghouses in Cape May County struggled to survive without their Southern guests.

In an effort to revive tourism, some ambitious entrepreneurs decided to promote horse racing. Joseph Heis, the owner of a hotel and stables, decided in 1866 to build a mile-long oval racetrack and clubhouse in Diamond Beach, an area situated between Cox Hall Creek and Town Bank. Named for the tiny stones that washed up on the beaches, which were polished and cut to resemble precious gems, Diamond Beach, with a hotel and several beach cottages, had attracted summer visitors since the 1840s. Heis and his partners formed the Diamond Beach Park and Hotel Association and purchased the ground in 1867. Construction of the track was completed in record time and the first sulky races were held there that summer. John West and Aaron Miller, owners of the United States Hotel in Cape May, were appointed managers of the track and clubhouse.

Although the racetrack eventually disappeared, the area remained a popular tourist destination through the 1960s. In the 1950s and '60s, a nightclub called the Playpen attracted a lot of celebrities during the summer. Tourists could enjoy a vacation stay at the Diamond Beach Motel located right next door. Both structures were torn down in the 1970s and replaced by a sea of condominiums, which are still standing today.

The Town Today

All remnants of the original Diamond Beach have been swept away in the tide of development that continues along the Jersey shore.

Directions

Situated just south of Wildwood Crest, you can reach Diamond Beach by taking the Garden State Parkway south to Route 109, then turning east on CR 621 (Ocean Drive).

GOSHEN

Cape May County's Land o' Goshen was home to many different industries after it was settled in the late seventeenth century.

History

What do whaling, crabbing, ship building, and cattle raising have in common? They were just a few of the industries that thrived at different times in the tiny town of Goshen. Aaron Leaming was the first person to begin raising cattle there in 1693. While he focused on making a living off the land, others turned their attention to the whales that swam in the deep waters of the Atlantic Ocean. Thomas Hand took up whaling after he migrated south from Long Island in the mid-1690s. He was so successful at the grueling trade that in 1699 he bought 340 acres of bayfront property from the West Jersey Society. His brother Benjamin, a farmer, bought 365 acres in Dennis Township while another brother, Shamgar, who had already made his fortune as a whaler on Long Island, moved to a seven-hundred-acre property in Middle Township in 1695.

By 1710, a small settlement had grown in Goshen. Residents who did not earn their living at sea worked in a crab-processing mill, while others ran lumber mills or built ships. The Tavern House, built around 1725 on what is now the corner of Route 47 and Goshen Landing Road, was one of the oldest original structures in the region. Through the years, it served as a tavern, hotel, dentist office, and private home. Much of the original woodwork, including hand-hewn logs and wooden rafter pegs, is still evident.

Between 1859 and 1898, the Garrison family built at least twenty-five sailing ships and smaller boats at their shipyard on Goshen Creek. Their business was unique because two ships could be constructed there at the same time; when they were finished, the vessels were slipped sideways into the water. The *Diamond* was the last ship launched there in 1898. Although shipbuilding in the region died out just a few years later, the dock pilings are still visible during low tide at the end of Goshen Landing Road.

The Site Today

While some new development has crept in, there are still some Colonial homes that reflect Goshen's thriving past, including that of J. P. Hand, a descendant of Thomas Hand, who has restored the farmhouse that has been in his family for generations.

Directions

Take Route 47 (Delsea Drive) south out of Millville. Goshen is located on Route 47 just west of the Beaver Swamp Fish and Wildlife Management Area.

RIO GRANDE

While neighboring Wildwood attracts millions of tourists each summer, the permanent population of Cape May County's Rio Grande never seems to grow to more than several hundred people.

History

Adventurous colonists were first attracted to the wilds of Cape May County in the late seventeenth century. Some sought freedom from religious persecution. Others, like Elizabeth Garlick, just hoped to find a place to hide. "Goody" (an abbreviation of the term "Goodwife") Garlick had left Long Island shortly after being arrested and accused of witchcraft. Her neighbors claimed that in addition to poisoning one family's child, she had soured the milk of someone else's cow. Although she was brought to court in Hartford, Connecticut, her accusers were not able to produce sufficient evidence against Garlick and the case was dismissed. She and her husband, John Parsons, fled to Cape May County in 1691 and eventually settled at the Leaming plantation, which later became the town of Rio Grande.

The couple lived quietly at the plantation for many years, where they raised Lydia, their only daughter. Interestingly enough, Goody Garlick's gravesite remains unknown. Is that because she eventually returned to practicing black magic and was banned from being buried in hallowed ground? While no one may ever know where her remains are located, some area residents say that each year during Halloween, a swirling white mist hovers over the wooded section of ground where her daughter is buried.

In the eighteenth century, Rio Grande was still home to the Leaming plantation and two others, owned by the Cress and Hildreth families. The Hildreths operated a general store at the intersection of King's Highway and the Dennisville road, where a stagecoach stop for travelers was also situated. Before long, the site was known as a trading post for local farmers, who would bring fresh produce to trade or sell. The area was referred to as Leamings by some, while others called it Hildreth. In the late 1800s, a descendant and namesake of the first Aaron Leaming who had read a book about Texas proposed Rio Grande, because he thought it sounded impressive. Others apparently agreed with him, because the new name for the town stuck after that.

In 1880, the state of New Jersey offered a bounty to encourage the production of sugarcane. The following year, local investors raised $250,000 and opened the Rio Grande Sugar Company, with George C. Potts serving as president. The company planned to raise its own sorghum, because local farmers didn't always deliver their cane in good condition for grinding. While a drought that same year made growing cane difficult, the following spring, about 1,000 acres of the 2,400 owned by the company were planted and liberally sprinkled with Peruvian guano, enriched with sulphate of ammonia. The company planted mostly amber cane, which ripened in three months, and the initial effort proved successful. Before long, local farmers were encouraged enough to grow cane as well.

The company employed 140 wagons and teams to cut and haul sorghum from Lemuel Miller's farm in Green Creek to the factory. The cane was brought by tramway to the mill, delivered already stripped of its outer coating, known as the begass, which became food for Miller's pigs. In 1883, Rio Grande produced 282,711 pounds of sugar and 55,000 gallons of molasses. Charles K. Landis, founder of nearby Vineland, Sea Isle City, and Hammonton, observed that the industry might prove a surprising success, but before long, the owners of the Rio Grande Sugar Company discovered they were spending more than they were making. The company went bankrupt and changed hands several times until it closed five years later. It 1889, the building became a cannery and later a slaughterhouse.

That same year, the state Department of Agriculture admitted that the region's soil would not produce high-quality cane and that their experiments proved "disappointing." Although the sugar industry didn't succeed, Rio Grande was an established town by that point, with residents who simply turned to other occupations to survive.

The Town Today

Since the 1970s, Rio Grande has been home to the *Cape May County Herald*, a local weekly newspaper. A quiet little community best known for the fishing, many of the homes and public buildings reflect its colonial past.

Directions

Take Route 9 south towards Cape May; Rio Grande sits just south of the intersection of Route 9 and Route 47 (Delsea Drive), southeast of Cape May County Park.

BIVALVE

Oysters Rockefeller and oysters on the half-shell—it's hard to believe that such gourmet treats enjoyed by the wealthy were once processed through shucking houses in the poor, isolated town of Bivalve in Cumberland County.

History

William Hollingshead Townsend was born on September 25, 1842, to Mark and Rachel (Garrison) Townsend, who lived between Dividing Creek and Port Norris. Growing up along the coast, where the locals fished daily, probably inspired Townsend's life calling. One of the first people to see the possibilities in harvesting oysters from the Delaware Bay, Townsend's oyster shipping business in the tiny community of Bivalve became very successful in the late nineteenth century after the Central Railroad of Jersey built a station there. By 1886, more than eighty cars of oysters were shipped daily from the appropriately named Bivalve, which was then considered the center of America's oyster industry. Hundreds of oyster schooners could be seen on the water each day, harvesting their catch.

One of Townsend's competitors was Capt. William B. Pepper, who was born in Dividing Creek on June 17, 1838, to Capt. Amos and Phoebe (Garrison) Pepper. Pepper was sent away to school at a young age, but when he turned ten, he started a seafaring career that lasted for twelve years. He later took command of an oyster boat, but when the Civil War broke out, he was enlisted in the Twenty-Fourth New Jersey Volunteer Infantry as a private. After participating in several major battles, Pepper was honorably discharged as a captain on July 3, 1863. He returned to operating an oyster boat for the next thirteen years, and after his retirement, he retained an interest in three boats. One of the founders of the Oyster Association, Pepper was also instrumental in having the railroad lines extended into Bivalve.

Around the turn of the twentieth century, a trolley line ran from Vineland to Bivalve with stops in Bridgeton and Millville. In 1904, the quiet community saw some unexpected activity when the U.S. Army Corps of Engineers hired Van Sant & Boehm of Atlantic City to remove the remains of the sloop *Constitution*, an oyster dredge boat, which lay sunk at the bottom of the Maurice River. The wreck, which had been impeding water traffic for many years, was blown up on July 27 after divers placed charges of dynamite along the ship. As the debris floated to the surface, local residents gathered various pieces of the ship for firewood. The keel, crossbeams, and other large pieces were transported by scow to the wharf at Bivalve and hauled away from there.

When America entered World War I in 1917, many young fishermen from Bivalve flocked to their local draft office to enlist. While they fought overseas, Bivalve remained one of the most important oyster shipping centers in the country. Many adults not directly employed by the industry spent their time harvesting salt hay, a popular insulation material used to protect everything from strawberries to poured concrete. Robert DuBois, a sailmaker, employed three men. James Muloey, another sailmaker, had two workers. Newcomb & Harker, the local shipwrights, employed seven men. Children attended the public school in neighboring Port Norris. Although township officials promoted the need at that time for an oyster canning plant, which could employ about fifty residents, no such industry was developed. But at the same time, hundreds of oyster-dredging schooners were built along the coast before the Great Depression forced a decline in the industry.

By the 1920s, the oyster business continued to thrive. Edward C. DuBois opened the first shucking house in Bivalve, where the oysters were opened before they went to market. Shortly afterward, J. T. McNaney of Maryland came north and opened a second house, bringing his own workers with him. Soon, other competitors entered the market, and by 1930, the local oyster shucking industry, which had started with eight workers at DuBois's plant, employed more than 1,200 people. Some racial tension arose when African Americans migrated to the town from Virginia and Maryland in search of work. They lived in row after row of tar paper shacks, without heat or running water. At that time, the Ku Klux Klan was attempting to raise support in New Jersey and tried without much success to intimidate them. Still, the KKK maintained a foothold in the region for many years. In 1938, they burned a cross in the front yard of Dr. Leonard Scott's home in Bridgeton. Scott, the only African-American doctor in the area, was not frightened by their actions. He continued to deliver babies and also tended to the needs of the oyster shuckers at his clinic in Port Norris. The doctor, who delivered nearly one thousand babies over the years, continued to make house calls at all hours until he retired in 1989 at age eighty-one.

Unfortunately, the oyster industry was shattered in 1957 when a parasitic disease called MSX (multinucleated sphere unknown) decimated the oyster population. With a high mortality, the oyster harvest fell from 711,000 bushels around 1957 to 49,000 bushels just three short years later. The oysters seemed to eventually develop some resistance to MSX, but in 1990, they were attacked by another parasite known as Dermo (*Perkinus marinus*). Although researchers raced to find a solution, the cause of the diseases remains undetermined even today. Some believed that the parasites traveled north from warmer southern waters, while others felt that pollution played a role in their development. In either instance, the existence of the diseases has prevented the local oyster industry from enjoying the same success it had in earlier years. But that didn't stop local businesses from trying. In 1982, six shucking houses remained open: Delaware Bay Oyster Company, Bivalve Packing Company, George O. McConnell, Port Norris Oyster Company, Reed and Reed, and King Oyster Farm.

The workers at that time still used the same basic methods to open the oysters that had been employed for more than fifty years. The oysters were individually placed on a wooden shucking block against a piece of metal, and then the thin outer edge of the shell was tapped to allow room for a knife to enter and sever the muscle holding the shell closed. With a twist of the wrist, the oyster was removed from the shell and dumped into a shucking pot. After they were washed and drained, the oysters were packed in different sized cans. At that time, the workers earned about $35 a week for a grueling day that usually started at 5:30 in the morning. In 1995, about one hundred thousand bushels of seed oysters were harvested, and of that number, about three thousand bushels went directly to market—the first since the late nineteenth century. Two years later, record harvests resulted in a production of more than $2 million in oysters.

The Town Today

While what remains of the local oyster business is now headquartered a few miles north in neighboring Port Norris, Bivalve is home to the *A. J. Meerwald*, a restored oyster dredging schooner that was launched in 1928. As of this writing, the ship is used by the Bayshore Discovery Project, offering onboard educational programs that promote a better understanding of the region's history and environment. The 85-foot *A. J. Meerwald*, which can carry forty-four passengers, was listed in 1995 in the National Register of Historic Places.

Directions

Take High Street south out of the town of Port Norris. It turns into the aptly named Shell Road. Follow Shell Road until it ends at the Maurice River. Only one private home still stands in Bivalve, which is located just south of the oyster shucking houses.

GREENWICH

Generations ago, Greenwich was the heart of Cumberland County, pulsing with life and activity. The bustling seaport, home to ship captains, farmers, and entrepreneurs, also held its own "tea party," just prior to the Revolutionary War.

History

Stand on any corner of Ye Greate Street, which runs through the town of Greenwich, and it's easy to imagine that the residents there still travel by horse and wagon. The homes along this main artery have changed little in three hundred years, and as far as the townspeople are concerned, that's exactly how they like it. History is treasured in Greenwich; in addition to preserving beautiful brick homes and impressive public buildings, the town is headquarters for the Cumberland County Historical Society, which protects everything from government records to individual objects, diaries, and journals.

Interestingly enough, the immigrants who founded Greenwich, or Cohansey, as it was known then, weren't really concerned about preserving the past—after all, they had sailed a thousand miles just to get away from their old lives. Greenwich on the Cohansey River was started in the late seventeenth century by John Fenwick, who welcomed Quakers, Baptists, and immigrants of different faiths who had not been accepted in other colonies. Settlement began in 1683, the same year that Deborah Swinney became the first child born among the colonists. The settlers planned to build a town that would be called Greenwich and feature a one-hundred-foot wide and two-mile long main street, a Friends meetinghouse, and Episcopal and Presbyterian churches. Between 1695 and 1765, Greenwich became an official port of entry into the New World. During that period, the town was well-known for the biannual fairs held each April and October. Farmers would cart their produce to town, while traders and crafters tried to interest area residents in their wares.

One of the oldest structures in town is the Gibbon House, built about 1730 by Nicholas Gibbon on a broad lot on Ye Greate Street. Constructed in a checkered pattern, the red bricks were reportedly imported from England, while the lighter-colored ones were made from local clay. Gibbon lived in the elegant three-story house, while his brother Leonard built a stone house a few miles away. The Gibbons were English immigrants who erected one of the first gristmills on the Macanippuck stream and later built a fulling mill on Pine Mount Run. Nicholas would later move to Salem County, where he served as sheriff from 1741 to 1748. After his death, his son Grant sold the house in Greenwich and eighteen acres of ground. In 1759, it was purchased by Richard Wood, a landowner whose holdings spread throughout West Jersey and whose descendants launched the chain of Wawa food stores.

The Stone Tavern, in the Dutch Colonial style, was built in Greenwich in 1734 of cut stone that was probably the ballast from a trading ship. The tavern, a popular meeting place, served as the first jail for local miscreants. By 1748, however, as the criminal element increased, the county board of chosen freeholders voted that year to erect a log jail in town. Criminals were transported to Greenwich, where their cases were tried before a magistrate.

In 1768, a ferry ran from John Sheppard's wharf to Back Neck, a location near the town of Millville. In 1771, Greenwich resident Richard Renshaw ran an advertisement in the *Pennsylvania Gazette* announcing that he had found a "bright sorrel mare" that he would be happy to return to its rightful owner. The trotter was described as having a "white mane and tail, a blaze down her face, her fore and hind feet white."

That same year, Michael Lee placed an announcement in the *Pennsylvania Journal*, thanking all of the local residents who used his stagecoach service. Lee's Cumberland Stage line was so successful that he bought a wagon large enough to comfortably hold twelve passengers. In his notice, he promised to maintain his schedule of leaving Seth Bowen's in Greenwich every Monday evening and Friday morning, transporting his passengers to Cooper's Ferry (later known as Camden).

Like many West Jersey towns, loyalties in Greenwich were divided prior to the outbreak of the Revolutionary War. Relatives and long-time friends sometimes found their relationships strained by arguments over loyalty to the crown versus America's right to be free of English rule. Tensions came to a head right before Christmas of 1774, when some Greenwich residents decided to stage their own tea-burning, just like the one that had occurred the year before in Boston harbor. They had little trouble finding a target, because the India Tea Company had made the mistake of directing the English brig *Greyhound*, helmed by Capt. J. Allen, to their harbor. The ship arrived in port on the night of December 12. Dan Bowen, a Loyalist, offered to store the cargo of tea it carried in his cellar while Allen figured out a way to transport it safely into Philadelphia.

Some of Bowen's neighbors were outraged by his actions and scheduled a town meeting for December 23, but on the preceding night, a small group of men gathered at Richard Howell's home in Roadstown, four miles north of Greenwich, and decided to impart their own brand of justice. After their meeting, the men returned to their town and gathered at the home of Rev. Philip Vickers Fithian. When they left a short time later, they disguised themselves as Indians, complete with war paint. Galloping up to Bowen's house, the men raided the cellar and piled the cartons of tea in the Market Square. They set fire to the stack, dancing around and cheering as it burned. L. Q. C. Elmer, a local historian, later wondered about their real motives, because a young partisan named Henry Stacks was seen cramming so much tea into his clothing that night, he "literally resembled a walking warehouse." Regardless of their intentions, some of the alleged conspirators were later brought to trial. Fortunately for them, no one was ever convicted since few local residents chose to speak about what they had seen that night.

With such a colorful past, is it any surprise that more than a few spectral residents still make their home in Greenwich? One of the most infamous spirits lurking within city limits is that of Pirate John, a privateer who, like Captain Kidd and Blackbeard, loved to roam Delaware Bay seeking out fresh prey. In the fall of 1721, John and his men were said to have gathered at his house in Greenwich to divide the spoils from their most recent sea raid. When John tried to claim more than his fair share of the booty as captain, the other pirates grabbed him, brutally beat him, and then divided his gold between them. They chained him to the brick floor where he died, moaning, several hours later. Local pets still avoid the Pirate House, as it is known, because John's ghost is said to linger there.

The spirit of Mary Maskell, a Quaker, is said to haunt Resurrection Hall, a property she received as part of her dowry when she married Thomas Ewing on March 20, 1720. After her death, overnight guests who stayed in an upstairs bedroom would wake to find a woman in gray standing silently by the bed for a few minutes before retreating into the shadows. Then there's little Amy, who once lived in the Pumpkin House on Ye Greate Street. Although the Pumpkin House is now painted a soft green rather than a deep orange color, it hasn't changed much from the days when Amy lived there in the 1840s. Her short life was abruptly ended by illness. For many years afterward, however, the child's spirit reportedly roamed through the house, playing pranks and childish games. Children who previously lived there often claimed to have spoken with Amy, but after one tenant decided to fill the attic with an assortment of stuffed animals and games, the little girl restricted her haunting to that area of the house.

The Town Today

Today, there is a monument to the Greenwich Tea Party in the center of town and many of the original houses still stand. The Cumberland

County Historical Society makes its home at the Gibbon House. The lower floor is furnished as a colonial home, with the second floor holding exhibits. Out back, there is a barn museum and an early Swedish log cabin. Special events are regularly hosted there throughout the year.

Directions

Follow CR 607 southwest out of Bridgeton. When it dead-ends at Ye Greate Street, you've arrived in Greenwich.

MAURICETOWN

South Jersey is dotted with tiny towns that have managed to avoid the crush of new development in recent years. Few have retained the charm of Mauricetown in Cumberland County, which sits on the banks of the Maurice River.

History

Mauricetown was settled about 1730 by John Peterson, a surveyor who mapped out the waterways that ran through what would later be called Commercial Township. Before 1789, Luke Mattox invested in so much property there that the place was eventually dubbed Mattox's Landing. It was the site where local settlers transported cordwood and lumber that was then shipped to larger cities. Business was so brisk that in 1803, George Elkinton built a wharf to accommodate all of the water traffic. Eleven years later, the Compton brothers bought up much of the land on the banks of the Maurice River, on which they laid out plots for homes. They renamed their settlement Mauricetown in honor of the waterway.

The name seemed only fitting since the water was the lifeblood of the community. Between 1846 and 1915, eighty-nine ship's captains made their home in Mauricetown, regularly leaving the tranquility of West Jersey for the lure of foreign ports. For months and sometimes years at a time, they traveled to exotic places like the West Indies, Europe, and South America, bringing home silks and satins and other treasures that would often become family heirlooms. Isaac Peterson was a captain who settled in town after he married Sarah Ann Lore on September 7, 1852. Peterson's house, a vernacular wood Italianate, still stands on Front Street. The seafarer often piloted his ship, the *Harry B. Ritter*, to the island of Martinique because he was reportedly fond of that Caribbean port.

Like many local captains, Peterson had his ship crafted in the shipyard of Joseph W. Vannaman & Brother, located at the base of South Street. In addition to larger seafaring vessels like the *Harry B. Ritter*, the *John D. Paige*, and the *Martha J.*, Vannaman later built the oyster schooners that plied their trade along the coast. Three of these schooners were renovated as passenger vessels in 1973: The *James H. Nixon* was built by Vannaman around 1873 and the *Isaac H. Evans* and the *Brenda Grace Walker* were both constructed in 1886. To facilitate production in the nineteenth century, John C. Weaver and some business associates opened a steam-powered sawmill at the shipyard. Between 1831 and 1901, more than fifty sailing ships were built in the small town.

Mauricetown's first post office opened on May 15, 1820, with John Hill serving as postmaster. On November 17, 1870, that position was taken over by Emma S. Howell. In 1880, the census determined that 575 people lived in the small coastal community.

The Town Today

Tranquil is the word that best describes Mauricetown, which has changed little over the past two hundred years. The Mauricetown United Methodist Episcopal Church is home to the Mariners Memorial Window, which lists the names of the captains and crew members who were lost at sea between 1856 and 1914. Although the general store portion is closed, local residents still get their mail in the building that housed it; it serves as the post office. They also spend their time keeping their Colonial and Victorian homes in pristine condition.

The Mauricetown Historical Society runs a small house museum that offers programs and activities for visitors and area residents.

Directions

Take Route 47 south out of Millville, through Port Elizabeth to the Mauricetown Crossway Road. Turn right and follow it to the intersection of CR 670 and Highland Street. Bear left onto Highland Street, which runs directly into Mauricetown.

OTHELLO AND SPRINGTOWN

Othello and Springtown in Cumberland County are two neighboring communities where African Americans who successfully escaped from Southern plantations via the Underground Railroad found sanctuary. Led to safety by fearless "conductors" like Harriet Tubman and protected by Quakers and other abolitionists, they in turn did their part to shelter others on the road to freedom.

History

Othello and Springtown are tiny villages about a mile apart, tucked away in a back pocket of rural Cumberland County. Settled in the mid-eighteenth century, as so many towns were in West Jersey, the residents were primarily free African Americans and escaped slaves. Although they were few in number at that time, the residents of Othello worked closely with the Sheppards, a Quaker family from Greenwich who were part of the Underground Railroad. The Sheppards, who owned the docks on the Cohansey River, helped fugitive slaves find their way to the church in Othello. From Othello, anyone who chose not to stay in town moved on to places like Swedesboro, Mount Holly, and Jersey City or points farther north. Harriet Tubman reportedly traveled to and from the Springtown station between 1849 and 1853. When slave catchers learned about the route across the Delaware Bay used by Tubman and other conductors, they would lie in wait at the water's edge. To elude them, the conductors used lanterns to warn travelers of any potential danger.

Springtown was originally established for the black farmhands who came north shortly after the Revolutionary War. When New Jersey passed the Manumission Act of 1786, many Quakers freed their slaves and sold them small tracts of land. In 1810, a Quaker named Thomas Maskell sold Ambury Hill in Othello to Jacob Bryant, a free man from Massachusetts, and Charles Lockerman for $100.

Until the early 1800s, both white and black Methodist Episcopals worshipped together in church, united by their opposition to slavery, but as some church leaders wavered on their antislavery stance, African Americans usually found themselves no longer welcome at Sunday services. They organized their own congregation in 1795 and built a church on Ambury Hill. In 1810, they formed the African Society of Methodists and purchased a small cabin where they worshipped. Seven years later, the congregation joined the newly chartered African Methodist Episcopal Church, which was formed in Philadelphia. Although the church is no longer standing, the cemetery at Ambury Hill includes the graves of Civil War veterans who served for the Union Army in the Colored Troops of Cumberland County. Among the African-American men buried there are Edward Staten and John Williams, who served in the 22nd Colored Regiment, which fought in Virginia.

By the advent of the Civil War, Springtown was a thriving community of free African Americans who strongly supported the abolitionist movement. Like neighboring Othello, the town became a stop on the Underground Railroad. While fugitive slaves escaping from the South sometimes passed through the town, preferring to move farther north, others chose to settle there. For many years, small, unpainted homes and a school stood in Springtown, surrounded by open fields that were farmed by the residents. After the church in Othello was destroyed by arsonists in the late 1830s, the congregation built a second church in Springtown in 1838, about two miles away from the original location at Ambury Hill. The new building was located next door to the home of Algy Stanford, a church member and Underground Railroad operator. Today, Bethel Othello African Methodist Episcopal Church is the oldest African Methodist Episcopal church in the state. It is one of the last churches in existence at which Richard Allen, the founder and first bishop of African Methodism, preached.

The Towns Today

By 1900, Othello was just another small town, its main street lined with neatly kept two-story wooden homes ringed by wooden fences; it has changed little since then. Unlike neighboring Springtown, however, it is still listed on state maps. There are very few historic homes left in Springtown, which sprawls just north of Othello. The interior of the Bethel Othello African Methodist Episcopal Church remains practically unchanged; the narrow staircase that leads to the second-floor choir loft shows the indentations where generations of feet have stepped.

Directions

To get to Othello, take CR 607 (Greenwich Road) southwest out of Bridgeton to CR 650 (Sheppards Mill Road). Turn right on 650 and follow it until it intersects with CR 623 (Ye Greate Street). Springtown is located northeast of Othello at the intersection of CR 650 (Sheppards Mill Road) and CR 620.

AURA

Aura in Gloucester County apparently was formed around a chapel that was built there in the early nineteenth century to welcome the Methodist circuit riders who rode from town to town, preaching on Sundays.

History

John Early, who migrated from Ireland to America in 1764, is believed to have been the first person to preach the Methodist doctrine in New

Jersey. At twenty-six, he settled on the Aura-Glassboro Road near Little Run Stream, where he built a sawmill. Early and his wife later raised nine children at their home near the town that was variously known as Old Union Church, Union, Unionville, and later, Union Grove or Union Station. Weekly meetings, which drew people from as far as fifty miles away, were first held at his log cabin. By 1806, a Methodist meetinghouse was built in town, and four years later, the church cemetery was started. In 1809, Francis Asbury, a Methodist circuit rider, preached at the two-story white church as he made his rounds through South Jersey. Early's log cabin survived for more than one hundred years before it was destroyed by fire. In 1878, the church was moved to its present location and rebuilt. In the years that followed, the congregation added a Sunday school building, with eight classrooms and a recreation hall.

The town was renamed Aura at the suggestion of John Tonkins, who served as postmaster in 1888. He wanted to avoid confusion with other towns in New Jersey that were named Union Station. The post office was first located in Locuson's general store and then was moved to Joe Gotti's store (later the front part of Nicholson's warehouse). In the nineteenth century, the town's chief employer was the Fork and Elevator Manufacturing Company, which produced hay forks. The business was operated by president and manager Jacob R. Fitzhugh, who also owned the general store, which was connected to a coal yard; later owned by Thomas McClure, Clement Gardiner, Linwood Locuson, and Vernon Nicholson, the store remained open until 1963. After it closed, the building became home to the Aura branch bank of The Peoples Bank of South Jersey. One local resident, Clerence Runge, recalled that in Aura's early days, miscreants were taken to Woodbury. There they would be tried and hanged near Rachor's Point at a place called Hangman's Hill.

Fitzhugh, descended from German immigrants, was one of the earliest settlers in Aura. Born on March 28, 1848, in Indiana County, Pennsylvania, he moved to New Jersey with his family when he was twenty-three. The Fitzhughs worshipped at the German Church, which later became the local Grange Hall, and then the town's municipal building. Joseph Guest and Nicholas Black organized the Aura Grange, which held its first meetings around 1911 on what was later the second floor of Nicholson's warehouse. The organization later moved to the Grange Hall about 1923 and purchased the building near the Aura-Hardinville Road from the German Church. To raise funds, the Grange operated a small store that sold items such as cocoa, coffee, and vanilla, but when membership fell a short time later, the state chapter ordered the Aura Grange to close.

In the early 1900s, the only business still in operation was the carriage and wagon building at F. S. Stewart & Sons, where four men were employed. By 1918, the Bridgeton branch of the West Jersey & Seashore Railroad had opened a station in the town of about two hundred residents. At that time, Aura had one public school consisting of four grades and the Methodist Church. The Aura Holiness Camp, which started then on Willow Grove Road, is still in operation today. The only fraternal organization in town at that time was a lodge of the Patrons of Husbandry. Farming had replaced hay forks as the town's major industry; the principal crops were white and sweet potatoes, tomatoes, strawberries, and a variety of fruit trees. Poultry was also an important industry of the town.

In 1932, three white oaks in the church cemetery were added to a register as being at least 250 years old, which meant they were part of the original forest cleared by William Penn and his followers. About 1945, the Aura post office was permanently closed.

The Town Today

Aura still offers a small-town atmosphere, but a number of housing developments have sprung up in recent years on the outskirts of town.

Directions

Follow Route 55 south to the Clayton-Aura Road and turn right. Aura is just a few miles from the highway, situated at the intersection of Ewan-Aura Road and Aura-Woodstown Road.

HARRISONVILLE

The developers of Harrisonville in Gloucester County once had big dreams for this tiny town.

History

Situated in the northwest corner of Harrison Township at the head of Oldman's Creek, a small stream that flows into the Delaware River, Harrisonville was considered by nineteenth-century standards to be a fairly large town. Only about nine houses stood there in 1835 when it was originally known as Coletown, or by the less refined name of Pig's Eye. They belonged to George Horner, Martha Cole, Israel Kirby, Samuel Cole, Nathan Gaunt, John Howey, William Mounce, Thomas Cole, Susan Pimm, and John Fogg, who opened the town's first general store. Nine years later, the town was renamed in honor of Gen. William Henry Harrison (1773–1841), the hero of Tippecanoe, who later became the ninth president of the United States. In 1848, James Saunders opened a store in the building that would later be occupied by Halderman & Hazelton's general store, while Isaac Lock started a business on a nearby corner in 1855. By 1875, Harrisonville was home to about thirty-five families, a water-powered sawmill, a gristmill that had been built in 1810 by Thomas Cole, some stores, and an Odd Fellows Hall. A schoolhouse sat on the edge of town.

In 1883, the mills were owned by Parker D. Lippincott, and Nathan Gaunt's wheelwright shop was run by William Ladow, who also served as one of three blacksmiths. The other two blacksmith shops were run by Amos Eastlack and the Pimm brothers. Lewis Amy was the local shoemaker there for more than thirty years. At that time, Halderman & Hazelton's general store competed for business against the Riggins brothers. William Matson, who had bought property from the Cole family when he arrived in town in 1846, worked for several years as a dealer in livestock and also ran a butchering business before taking up farming. Dr. Samuel Stanger looked after the medical needs of the residents of Harrisonville.

In 1918, about three hundred people lived in the town. The nearest train station for the West Jersey & Seashore Railroad was located a little more than three miles away.

Harrisonville had one school and a Methodist Episcopal church but numerous fraternal orders, including the Odd Fellows, Knights of Pythias, and a Grange of Patrons of Husbandry. Town officials hoped that investors would start a canning factory or a creamery to employ local residents, but no such industry ever opened there. The gristmill, which had been a fixture in the town for more than one hundred years, was still in operation at that time.

Although the creek had been initially dammed to make it a source of waterpower for the mills, by the early twentieth century, the lake was popular with local residents, who fished there for bass, pickerel, yellow perch, and catfish.

The Town Today

By 2000, census records indicated that the town's small population had dwindled still further to about 153 residents.

Directions

Harrisonville stands at the intersection of CR 617 and Ferrell Road, northeast of Woodstown.

PLAINVILLE

Pity poor Plainville! If it wasn't for the Plainville United Methodist Church, no one would even have a clue as to where this Gloucester County town once stood.

History

On August 25, 1823, Philip Woolford bought a tract of land from George Cake on the south side of the Indian Branch of the Maurice River and started a settlement that would become known as Woolfordtown. It was then renamed Trimmeltown, in honor of John

Trimmel, who was a millwright and respected as one of the best mechanics in the county. After that, it was called Hopeville, until somebody apparently decided that the collection of twelve homes around the Methodist church really didn't need anything but the most basic name and dubbed the town Plainville.

Fifty years after its founding, Plainville still hadn't grown, but attendance remained strong at the Methodist church on Marshall Mill Road. Area residents first worshipped at the Hopewell School on Tuckahoe Road, about a mile from the site where the church was built. The ground for the church was purchased for $50 from Robert and Elizabeth Wilson of Williamstown. John Trimel cut the wood for the church from his property and donated the lumber. The simple white structure first opened its doors for services in 1872. Seventeen years later, church trustees were able to pay the mortgage in full. For many years, a circuit rider, as Methodist preachers were known, offered mass at the church, which was one of five stops he made in South Jersey. Between 1900 and 1930, the church was frequently the site of revival meetings that sometimes lasted for days.

The Town Today

Plainville is considered a part of Elk Township these days. Inside the simple church, plain white pews line the aisles, while the white walls bear no decoration. As of 2010, mass was still offered every Sunday.

Directions

Take Route 47 (Delsea Drive) south to CR 659 (Marshall Mill Road). Turn left and go about five miles; look for the church on the right, standing on a slight rise. The cemetery is directly behind the church.

BARNEGAT LIGHT

Question: When is a ghost town not a ghost town? Answer: When, like Barnegat Light in Ocean County, it is annually deluged in the summer months by thousands of beach-loving tourists.

History

Stand on the portion of Long Beach Island known as Barnegat Light in the summer, and it is hard to imagine how it must look in the off-season, when just a little more than seven hundred people live there. Harder still to imagine what life was like back at the time when it was first sighted in 1609 by English explorer Henry Hudson, when the Native Americans were the island's only occupants. Five years after it was discovered by the English, the region was christened Barendegat, or "Inlet of the Breakers" by Dutch settlers because of its turbulent waters.

One of the area's first industries was whaling, which was encouraged by the Proprietors of New Jersey in the late seventeenth century as a way to attract settlers to the region. Although whaling never succeeded, the colonists who settled there were able to hunt enough game, catch enough fish, and dig enough oysters to make a profit. By the early 1700s, there were a handful of families scattered through the island, many of whom started cutting down timber that was sold to sawmills on the mainland. By the 1730s, a number of mills opened in Barnegat; business remained so brisk that Cranberry Inlet was opened in 1750 to provide a shortcut for cargo ships carrying goods to and from the island.

For many years, it was not uncommon for sailing ships to crash along the treacherous shoreline. In 1770, the *New-York Journal* ran a notice that the ship *Edward* from London, with Captain Kemble at the helm, ran aground on the beaches there. While the ship was believed to be lost, all of the passengers and cargo were saved. Kemble apparently got too close to the shore because he mistook Barnegat for "the Nevesinks, near the Hook."

During the Revolutionary War, American forces clashed with the British in Barnegat Light over a stranded cargo ship. On October 26, 1782, a beached Belgian cutter was discovered by Capt. Andrew Steelman of the privateer galley *Alligator*, who gathered together his crew and a group of local men to salvage its valuable cargo of tea that had been headed to the West Indies. As they were unloading the ship, the men were attacked by a band of Loyalists led by Capt. John

Bacon. More than twenty of Steelman's men died during what would later become known as the Barnegat Light Massacre.

Although the island had been occupied by European immigrants for close to a century, Caleb Parker, the first permanent settler, did not arrive in Barnegat until 1795. Within a few years, the region was popular with tourists for its hunting and fishing. In 1814, Bart and Ruth Slaight were among the first to build small homes on the beaches and lowlands. About ten years later, the Slaights constructed a larger house so that they could take in boarders. Their boarding-house was later sold to Jacob Herring, and the Herring House (as it became known) was popular with hunters from Philadelphia and New York. Worried even then about overdevelopment on the island, in 1834 the Slaights sold five acres of unspoiled ground to the federal government with the promise that it would remain pristine.

While the region wasn't seriously threatened by overdevelopment at that time, it did face a population explosion—of cats. A number of tailless Manx cats, which were being transported by ship to America, swam to safety along with the crew when their ship crashed off the coast. The cats quickly went feral, avoiding all contact with humans. They made a home for themselves in the heavy underbrush along the sand dunes and fed on fish, seagulls, and other shorebirds. Their population grew dangerously larger by the late nineteenth century, when members of the Life-Saving Service brought over domestic felines from the mainland. Although hunting parties attempted to kill off the feral cats, they continued to thrive for many years.

John M. Brown bought much of the land that made up Barnegat Light in 1855. Not surprisingly, he christened the town Brownsville and the Herring House was renamed the Ashley House. Since shipwrecks were still common, the community built a shelter there for victims. Around 1872, the United States Life-Saving Service built Station #17 in the area. Unfortunately, the Browns' son drowned at sea and they left the island shortly afterward. Their holdings were sold at auction in 1869. Five years later, the Ashley House was purchased by Charles Martin. Around that same time, a general store and post office were constructed near the intersection of 4th Street and Central

Avenue. In 1881, Benjamin Franklin Archer and some associates formed the Barnegat City Improvement Company to promote the town as a tourist destination. The company laid out the present pattern of streets, blocks, and lots in the town that was then called Barnegat City. Before long, crowds came from New York and Trenton by train to Toms River and from there to the island by boat.

By the late 1800s, the town had a number of hotels, including the Oceanic and the Sunset, both of which were managed by the Archer family. The Oceanic Hotel, located on East 4th Street, was washed away in 1919. The Sunset Hotel, located on West 5th Street, burned down in 1932. The Ashley House, sold to John Warner Kinsey in 1882, was reincarnated as the Kinsey Hotel. In 1886, the railroad built a bridge that established a direct line to Barnegat, providing easier access for tourists. Another bridge was opened at the south end of the town in 1914 to allow cars to travel between the island and the mainland. As violent storms and the tides continued to erode the shoreline, however, Barnegat lost its appeal for many tourists who turned instead toward the glitzier temptations of Atlantic City. Even the population, never large, diminished to just a little more than one hundred people in the 1930s.

Barnegat City, long a part of Long Beach Township, was incorporated in 1904 as a separate entity. In November 1948, its name was changed to Barnegat Light to reflect the significance of its most important landmark, the Barnegat Lighthouse. The first lighthouse was built in 1824 where Barnegat Bay merged with the Atlantic Ocean. Twenty years later, erosion had eaten away the soil beneath the lighthouse and it tumbled beneath the ocean waves. Realizing the need to protect that portion of the coastline, the U.S. Congress appropriated $6,000 for the construction of a second lighthouse three hundred feet south of the original location. Barnegat Light was completed in 1858; the new lighthouse was 150 feet tall and had a seventeen-foot high light chamber for the beacon that had been specially built in France. Barnegat Lighthouse, commissioned on January 1, 1859, is the second-tallest lighthouse in the United States. It remained in operation through 1927.

The Town Today

Barnegat Light is still very popular with fishermen, although foreign ships virtually wiped out the cod that once flourished in the surrounding waters. But even more significant is Old Barney, as the lighthouse is affectionately known; it draws thousands of visitors annually to Barnegat Lighthouse State Park on the northern tip of the island. The Barnegat Light Museum is housed in the town's original one-room school and features the original lens used in the lighthouse. The park, owned and operated by the state's Division of Parks and Forestry, is also home to a forest where birdwatchers gather to watch migrating species.

Directions

Take the Garden State Parkway to Exit 63 (Route 72 East). From there, turn left onto Long Beach Boulevard and follow the signs.

DOUBLE TROUBLE

Although they may not have been looking for it, some settlers found Double Trouble when they moved to Ocean County in the eighteenth century.

History

Anthony Sharp was a Quaker who fled England for Ireland in the seventeenth century to escape religious persecution. Although he never migrated to the New World, Sharp, a wool merchant who settled in Dublin, was later appointed one of the East Jersey Proprietors after William Penn began buying land throughout the state. After he received a grant of land, Sharp sent his nephew, Thomas, to America to supervise his holdings. When Sharp died, his son Isaac inherited a large part of his properties. The tract that would later become known as Double Trouble may have been purchased from Isaac around 1765 by Thomas Potter, who built a sawmill there on Cedar Creek. Potter, who ironically enough owned land around a town called Good Luck, known today as Lanoka Harbor, apparently succeeded at his new venture. The mill converted the surrounding forest of Atlantic white cedar trees into timber that was used into the early 1900s to build homes throughout the region.

Double Trouble was situated on high ground between two great bogs, which would later be named the Gowdy Bog (to the east) and Old Mill Pond Bog (to the west). How did the town gain its unique name? There are two different stories: the first explains that Thomas Potter declared he had "double trouble" after spring rains washed out the sawmill's dam not once but twice. Another more colorful tale claims that local muskrats, who were always gnawing away at the dam, chewed two holes in it at the same time one day, forcing a local minister who lived near the dam to holler that the town was in for double trouble.

In 1832, William Giberson, a sea captain, bought the property and is believed to have established the first cranberry bog at Double Trouble. About thirty years later, Ralph B. Gowdy bought the ground where the sawmill stood and started another cranberry bog there. Gowdy, a captain in the Union army, would raise a company of one hundred Ocean County volunteers during the Civil War.

In 1904, Edward Crabbe bought Double Trouble and began closing down the sawmill and lumbering operation. Five years later, he and George Bunker started the Double Trouble Company, which planted more than two hundred acres of cranberries for processing between 1910 and 1925. The bog became the largest in the state, and the town became one of New Jersey's largest cranberry producers. Inside the cranberry sorting and packing house were three cranberry separators, which helped lines of workers who manually sorted the cranberries.

At that time, about ten families lived in Double Trouble, including the Downings, the Pomeliers, the Platts, and the Newmans. Hiram Downing was a farmer who resided with his wife, Martha, and their three children, Jennie, nineteen, Lizzie, fifteen, and Hugh, age eleven. They had a live-in, sixteen-year-old cook named Hester Hildens.

By 1939, cranberries remained the town's main industry; Double Trouble's small population boomed in the fall when migrant workers arrived to help with the harvest. The state of New Jersey bought the Double Trouble Company from the Crabbe family in 1964 and leased some of the bogs to local cranberry farmers. The town became part of Double Trouble State Park, more than eight thousand acres of property owned and operated by the New Jersey Department of Environmental Protection's Division of Parks and Forestry.

The Town Today

The Double Trouble Historic District occupies more than two hundred acres within the state park. It features about fourteen buildings, including workers' homes, the mill, a cranberry packing house, and a school. The sawmill was restored in 1995, and work on the cranberry packing house was completed the following year. As of this writing, the cranberry bogs were leased to the New Jersey Devil Cranberry Company, which is currently renovating them. Visitors who tour the site in the fall can witness the annual harvest.

Directions

On the Garden State Parkway north, take exit 77. Turn left onto CR 618 west; go under the Parkway and travel approximately one-half mile on Pinewald-Keswick Road until you reach the traffic signal at Double Trouble Road. The park entrance is on the left.

ALLIANCE

This tiny town in Salem County was started in the nineteenth century as an agricultural community for Jewish émigrés who had escaped the pogroms in Russia.

History

After Czar Alexander II of Russia was assassinated in 1881, his efforts to reform some of his country's medieval practices, such as serfdom, were terminated by his successors. Russian Jews were targeted as the cause of many of the country's problems and they were often the victim of pogroms, violent organized attacks that were sanctioned by the aristocracy. In response, many Jewish families were forced to flee their homeland in the hope of finding safety and religious freedom in America.

After settling in overcrowded cities like New York, some Jewish immigrants decided to try farm life. A group, led by men like Moses Bayuk, organized the Alliance Colony, which opened on May 10, 1882. Named after the Alliance Israelite Universelle of Paris, the agricultural community was funded by the Hebrew Immigrant Aid Society of New York and Philadelphia and the Baron De Hirsch Fund. The Hebrew Immigrant Aid Society had previously given Bayuk a large parcel of land on the Maurice River, close to the train station in the nearby town of Norma. The property became the foundation for the Alliance Colony, which was initially settled by twenty-five people. Within a few months, more than sixty families made their home there.

Each family of settlers was given forty acres of tree-filled farmland that needed to be cleared. Despite their good intentions, this was a problem, because many of the newcomers had little experience in working the land. Fortunately, the Aid Society provided each family with a stipend while the forest was toppled, and other local farmers lent a hand, teaching the newcomers to plow and plant. In addition to farming, the residents supported themselves with blacksmithing, masonry, and cabinetmaking. Local officials provided them with army tents while permanent housing was built. The settlers worked hard to make their community a success and by 1901, there were about five hundred people living on close to two thousand acres at Alliance. In addition to their homes, the residents built four synagogues, several schools, and a small clothing factory, and established a Jewish cemetery.

The Town Today

While the residents of the Alliance Colony eventually dispersed, the cemetery is still used by Jewish residents of Cumberland and Salem

Counties. One remaining synagogue is open for special occasions. As of this writing, the Jewish Federation of Cumberland County is maintaining the home of Moses Bayuk, with plans to turn the property into a cultural center and museum. The old Tifereth Israel synagogue was built in 1889 in the vernacular style, which meant that local materials were used in its construction.

Directions

Take Route 55 south to CR 674 (West Garden Road). Turn right, staying on Garden Road to Henry Avenue. Turn left; Alliance is located at the intersection of Henry Avenue and Isaacs Avenue.

ALLOWAY

This community was the home of America's first successful glass factory, operated by Casper Wistar and his descendants for close to forty years prior to the American Revolution.

History

The town that would later be known as Alloway was originally christened Thompson's Bridge for Benjamin Thompson, a wealthy landowner who invested heavily in South Jersey. Settled in the seventeenth century by colonists like Jonathan House, who built one of the first homes there, Thompson's Bridge then became Allowaystown. One of its most prominent families was the Oakfords, who built three hip-roofed houses in the town. In 1767, William Oakford ran a newspaper advertisement warning area residents that a "Dutch Servant Man, named John Erhard Schlagel" had run away on May 17. He described Schlagel as being about thirty years old with long dark brown hair, grey eyes, and wearing a "redish brown" cloth coat, two linen shirts, and a felt hat. A large scar ran down the right side of his face from the corner of his eye to his mouth. Oakford offered to pay thirty shillings reward for Schlagel's return and warned "All Masters of Vessels are forbid to carry him off at their Peril." On December 2, 1772, Isaac Oakford advertised the following property for sale in the *Pennsylvania Gazette*: "A Valuable Plantation and Tract of Land, containing 250 acres . . . there is on said place, a good brick house, with barn, stabling and other out-houses." According to Isaac, the plantation was also home to a water-powered sawmill "lately rebuilt."

Allowaystown quickly attracted several mills because its location next to Alloways Creek made waterpower easily accessible. One of its earliest and most significant industries was the Wistarburgh Glassworks, situated just outside of town and opened in 1739 by a German immigrant named Caspar Wistar. Born in Hilsbach, Germany, on February 3, 1696, Wistar decided to seek his fortune in America when he turned twenty-one. After arriving in Philadelphia in 1717, he worked at a variety of trades but eventually prospered as a brass button maker and land speculator. Wistar became a British subject in 1724 and two years later joined the Religious Society of Friends, more commonly known as the Quakers. In 1727, he married Catherine Jansen, the daughter of a wealthy Quaker merchant, and they had seven children. Around 1739, Wistar started a glass factory just outside of Allowaystown. Using the vast pine forests for fuel and the silica sand as a key ingredient, Wistarburgh Glass Works produced tableware in a color that would become known as Jersey green—clear with a slight green tint.

The glasshouse remained in business for almost forty years, turning out handblown milk pans, pitchers, and even window glass. Its production caught the attention of the English crown, which demanded to know why Wistarburgh glass was not being exported, as was then required by law. Richard Wistar, who had taken over the glassworks after his father died in 1752, was no doubt grateful when Governor William Franklin, Benjamin's son, interceded and told the British that the glass made there was of poor quality and not worth transporting to England.

No one is certain exactly when or why Wistarburgh closed, although its furnaces apparently went out of blast by the advent of the Revolutionary War. When the glassblowers dispersed to neighboring towns like Glassboro, Allowaystown simply turned its attention to other businesses. Shipbuilding became one of the town's most important industries: In 1839, the *Stephen Baldwin*, a 650-ton ship, was launched at the Reeves Shipyard. Her keel measured 140 feet, with a 31-foot, 6-inch beam, and a hold that was 21 feet, 6 inches in size. The shipyard employed about seventy-five workmen and produced about $20,000 worth of ship timber every three months.

Although their store is no longer standing, Samuel Keen and Thomas Guest were two of the town's first merchants. While there is no record of who ran the first tavern in Allowaystown, James Ray operated a brick hotel there. But business was occasionally interrupted by the unexpected. On July 17, 1820, local residents watched, astounded, as a balloon carrying a single passenger that had departed Camden two hours earlier descended into a marsh at Alloways Creek around 7 P.M. William Bacon was the community's first doctor; after retiring from medicine in 1830, his practice was taken over by Dr. Thomas J. Yarrow, who treated local residents until his death in July 1882.

By 1876, Allowaystown had a population of about eight hundred residents, living in about one hundred homes along the creek and Diament's Mill Pond. It was also home to three general stores, a gristmill, and two hotels on Greenwich Street, as well as a post office, a cabinetmaker, a blacksmith shop, a tin shop, two churches (one Baptist and one Methodist), and three schools. The Salem branch of the West Jersey Railroad ran nearby. Seven years later, the town's name had been shortened to Alloway, but it was still considered "one of the most enterprising towns of its size in Salem County." Although its population had decreased to about six hundred, it provided residents with a variety of services that included three general stores, three butchers, four blacksmiths, two wheelwright shops, one milliner, and one hotel, along with a chair manufacturer, a brush manufacturer, and one lumberyard. At that time, the health of the townspeople was cared for by doctors Lemuel Wallace and W. Lloyd Ewen.

The Town Today

Standing on a corner at the heart of Alloway, it is difficult not to feel the ghosts of its industrial past. The homes and businesses are mostly eighteenth and nineteenth century; some are well cared for while others appear to be abandoned to time and neglect. Although Alloway never lived up to the prediction that it would become "the greatest manufacturing town in West Jersey," its rich history has provided modern-day researchers with vital clues to understanding the region's past.

In 1998, the Wheaton Arts and Cultural Center (then known as Wheaton Village) sponsored an archeological dig on the privately owned property where the glassworks once stood. Using a magnetometer, surveyors were able to determine that the factory's foundation still existed underground. They also found furnace brick, an ash pile, pot fragments, and a cullet pile at the site. Since the time of the dig, however, the owners of the property have declined all requests to conduct further investigations there.

Directions

Take Route 49 south out of the city of Salem. Turn left on Quinton-Alloway Road, which will run straight into town.

HANCOCK'S BRIDGE

Tucked away in a corner of rural Salem County, Hancock's Bridge was the site of a bloody massacre of American militiamen during the Revolutionary War.

History

Long before tragedy struck Hancock's Bridge, it was just a typical West Jersey town, filled with hardworking residents who plied a variety of trades, including those of miller, blacksmith, and carpenter. Predominantly Quaker, the community's location on Alloways Creek, just five miles south of the bustling city of Salem, gave it easy access to Philadelphia and Wilmington, two major American cities during the eighteenth century. Business was brisk, but when the colonists decided it was time to fight for their independence, Hancock's Bridge willingly sent its men off to war. Although few Revolutionary War battles were fought in the region, local residents soon found themselves haunted by a slaughter that occurred there one spring day.

On March 18, 1778, more than one thousand British troops ambushed about three hundred Salem militiamen at Quinton's Bridge, a small settlement just a few miles from the city of Salem. The Americans had hoped to keep the English from crossing the bridge over Alloways Creek to prevent them from raiding local farms for supplies. About forty Americans reportedly died in the skirmish, some drowning in the creek as they fled. The British force was led by Col. Charles Mawhood, the commander who had lost the Battle of Princeton to Gen. George Washington the year before. While Mawhood had been sent to West Jersey to find food for the British and Hessian troops in Philadelphia, his subordinates were eager to fight the Yankees.

The following day, Mawhood threatened to burn Salem and turn the women and children over to the Tories if the Americans did not surrender. In response, Col. Asher Holmes, commander of the Salem County militia, warned there would be immediate retaliation on Tory families in the area if anything happened to the wives and children of his men. While Mawhood appeared to back down, two days later, the same contingent of British troops surprised the militia a few miles away at Hancock's Bridge. The attack was led by Col. John Simcoe, the twenty-six-year-old commander of the Queen's Rangers, an elite battalion of veteran fighters. The farmers and merchants who comprised the militia did not stand a chance against professional soldiers.

In a driving rain, the British forces surrounded the elegant brick home of Judge William Hancock shortly after midnight. The Americans had commandeered the house from Hancock, who supported the Loyalist cause. Built in 1734 for the Hancocks, the house featured a blue-glazed pattern with the year of construction and the couple's initials "W," for William, and "S," for Sarah, woven into the brick.

Although William had died in 1762, he left the house to his son and namesake, who was also a judge. The Englishmen bayoneted the two sentries who stood outside the house, then broke in through the back and front doors to surprise the squad of militiamen who slept there. At least twenty Americans were killed that night, some after they tried to surrender, along with the judge and his brother, who had returned to the house in an effort to protect the property from the raiders. Simcoe and his Rangers then plundered the town before sailing back to Philadelphia.

Although the night of the massacre haunted Hancock's Bridge, its pragmatic population and their descendants soon got back to business when the war ended. By 1883, the town was prospering. In addition to a post office, a Friends meetinghouse, a Methodist church, a tavern, and a canning establishment, it was home to two stores and a growing number of residents. Local farmers brought their produce to Hancock's Bridge, where James Butcher and Lewis Carll shipped it to other cities and towns. An undertaker and a furniture shop were located there, along with a blacksmith and wheelwright shop. The blacksmith shop was once run by William Dunn, but by 1883, Joseph Powelton and John Sheppard had operated the business for ten years.

Three businesses, opened at Hancock's Bridge at various times, were known as the "upper," "middle," and "lower" stores. Among the merchants who ran the upper store were Thomas Reeves, John H. Lambert, William Bradway, and Edward Carll. Some occupants of the middle store included Charles Mulford, James Bradway, and Abner Fox. The lower store also had a variety of occupants before 1859, but that year was taken over by William E. Scudder. William Hancock and Joseph Thompson, who once owned businesses in Salem County, were killed in the Hancock House massacre.

The Town Today

Hancock's Bridge is a state-owned historic site operated by the Division of Parks and Forestry. The Hancock House is a museum that provides background on the events that occurred there during the Revolutionary War.

Directions

Take Route 49 south out of the city of Salem. Follow that to Keasbey Street; turn right and Keasbey Street becomes Yorke Street. Follow Yorke Street south past Evergreen Cemetery, at which point Yorke becomes Hancock's Bridge Road. Stay on Hancock's Bridge Road south; go over a small bridge that will take you right into the town.

OAKWOOD BEACH

The town of Oakwood Beach in Salem County was started as a summer colony in the late nineteenth century.

History

Mention the Jersey shore and most people automatically think of the sandy stretch of coastline that fronts the Atlantic Ocean from Island Beach to Cape May. The west coast of South Jersey is usually all but forgotten except for a handful of local residents and avid fishermen, who enjoy the serenity of the Delaware River on a warm summer's day. They were not the first to appreciate that section of the coastline, however. The region was first settled by Swedish colonists in the mid-seventeenth century, but they were eventually ousted by English Quakers led by John Fenwick, who laid claim to thousands of acres there.

The section of the coast where Oakwood Beach is situated later attracted its fair share of attention because of its proximity to major cities such as Wilmington and Philadelphia. The town was named for the huge oak trees that dotted the coast, which were used to build wooden sailing ships in the early 1800s at the Philadelphia Navy Yard. Oakwood Beach was a popular summer resort by the end of the nineteenth century. A belief in the natural healing property of fresh air and sunshine attracted visitors from New Jersey, Delaware, and Philadelphia. The first cottages were built along its sandy shore in the 1890s, and a dance hall and pavilion soon followed. In later years, two country clubs, complete with golf courses, were added. The summer cottages remained standing into the 1930s. Farming was a major occupation into the early 1900s; on numerous occasions, plows turned up evidence of Native American campsites, including arrowheads and grooved axes.

The Town Today

Oakwood Beach is no longer just a summer colony. New housing has sprung up in recent years, and many of its eighteenth- and nineteenth-century buildings are gone. The Samuel Nicholson House, built in 1752, still stands on Oakwood Beach Road. Only one golf course is still in business. The pavilion was located near where the Owl Inn stands today.

Directions

Follow Route 49 west and then turn left on Route 625. Oakwood Beach is situated on the Delaware Bay just north of Fort Elfsborg and south of Sinnickson Landing.

SHIRLEY

Surrounded by rolling fields, Shirley is situated at a crossroads deep in the heart of rural Salem County.

History

When twenty-three-year-old Samuel Swing (1732–1801) migrated to America from France in 1755 with his brother Jeremiah, he was filled with curiosity about this new land that was creating such interest in Europe. The Swings were wealthy world travelers who had meandered around Europe for many years but ultimately decided to settle when they reached the New World. Samuel moved to Long Island, where he met and married Sarah Diamant, the daughter of Nathaniel and Lois Diamant. After their wedding, the young couple headed south into the wilds of West Jersey, a region that was attracting other

French émigrés. They were accompanied by Jeremiah, who stayed for four years to help them clear the land, plant their crops, and build houses for other settlers, before moving out to western Pennsylvania.

The Swings constructed an elegant red-brick home for themselves in the Dutch style, complete with the date of its completion, 1775, and the initials, SSS, for Samuel and Sarah Swing, set in white brick on one side. They joined the Pittsgrove Presbyterian church in nearby Daretown when they moved to West Jersey. Swing, a devout man, was apparently an early believer in the abolition of slavery. When Robert Ward and Samuel Pennington of Maryland appeared on his doorstep one day in the spring of 1797, claiming to be on the trail of several escaped slaves, Swing refused to cooperate with them even though he had in fact sheltered at least one of the men they were seeking. West Jersey had outlawed slavery by that time and Ward and Pennington were warned they would not receive assistance, no matter who they approached for help.

The Swings raised six children at their bucolic Salem County home. As they married, the Swings provided them with property along a well-traveled crossroads in Upper Pittsgrove Township that was eventually dubbed Swing's Corner. In addition to their homes, the hamlet contained a general store and several shops where wheelwrights and blacksmiths plied their trades. Other families soon moved to the region, which became known for its rich annual potato and grain harvests. For many years, Swing's Corner remained large enough to maintain a post office and its general store. In the early nineteenth century, however, the locals decided to rename their small community Shirley, in honor of a very popular novel written in 1849 by author Charlotte Brontë.

The Town Today

While the post office closed in the early twentieth century, the name Swing's Corner remained interchangeable with that of Shirley for many years. None of Samuel and Sarah's descendants live in the immediate area, but members of the Swing family still reside in South Jersey. About five farms, devoted to dairy farming and growing grain and potatoes, remain in operation in Shirley. While the general store still stands at the crossroads, it was empty at the time of this writing. The Colonial brick home of Samuel and Sarah Swing, which is located north of town, is still a private residence. The Swings and many of their descendants are buried nearby at the Pittsgrove Presbyterian Church. Listed in the National Register of Historic Places, the church was built in 1767 on a rise overlooking Daretown Road in Daretown. Once a training college for young men who wanted to be ministers, two companies of soldiers were formed there during the Revolutionary War; they fought against British and Hessian troops at Philadelphia and Mount Holly. Services are no longer held at the church on a regular basis.

Directions

Shirley is located at the intersection of Route 77 (Pole Tavern Road) and Shirley Road, southwest of Elmer.

BIBLIOGRAPHY

Books and Articles

Adams, Charles J. *Atlantic County Ghost Stories*. Reading, PA: Exeter House Books, 2003.

Andrews, Bessie Ayars. *Colonial and Old Houses, of Greenwich, New Jersey*. Vineland, NJ: Vineland Historical and Antiquarian Society, 1907.

Badger, Curtis J. *The Wild Coast: Exploring the Natural Attractions of the Mid-Atlantic*. Charlottesville: University of Virginia Press, 2005.

Bastien, Jan Lynn. *Ghosts of Mount Holly: A History of Haunted Happenings*. Charleston, SC: History Press, 2008.

Beck, Henry Charlton. *Forgotten Towns of Southern New Jersey*. New Brunswick, NJ: Rutgers University Press, 1961.

———. *The Jersey Midlands*. New Brunswick, NJ: Rutgers University Press, 1962.

———. *More Forgotten Towns of Southern New Jersey*. New Brunswick, NJ: Rutgers University Press, 1963.

———. *The Roads of Home: Lanes and Legends of New Jersey*. New Brunswick, NJ: Rutgers University Press, 1956.

Buchan, Perdita. *Utopia, New Jersey: Travels in the Nearest Eden*. New Brunswick, NJ: Rivergate Books, 2007.

Combination Atlas Map of Salem and Gloucester Counties, New Jersey. Chicago: Everts & Stewart, 1876; reprint, Woodbury, NJ: Gloucester County Historical Society, 1970.

Crowley, Bill. *Bill Crowley Recalls Stories of Old Ironia*. Self-published: n.d.

Cunningham, John T. *New Jersey: America's Main Road*. Garden City, NY: Doubleday, 1976.

———. *The New Jersey Sampler: Historical Tales of Old New Jersey*. Upper Montclair: New Jersey Almanac, 1964.

Cushing, Thomas, and Charles E. Sheppard. *History of the Counties of Gloucester, Salem, and Cumberland, New Jersey, with Biographical Sketches of their Prominent Citizens*. Philadelphia: Everts & Peck, 1883.

Dorwart, Jeffrey M. *Cape May County, New Jersey: The Making of an American Resort Community*. New Brunswick, NJ: Rutgers University Press, 1993.

Federal Writers' Project. *New Jersey: A Guide to its Present and Past*. New York: Hastings House, 1939.

Flemming, George D. *Brotherton*. Medford, NJ: Plexus Publishing, 2005.

Fowler, Horace N., and Samuel T. Fowler. *The Industrial Public: A Plan of Social Reconstruction in Line with Evolution*. 1921; reprint, Whitefish, MT: Kessinger Publishing, 2009.

Hinds, William Alfred. *American Communities and Co-operative Colonies*. 1908; reprint, General Books, 2010.

Johnson, Arthur L. *The Deserted Village*. Elizabeth, NJ: Union County Park Commission, 1947.

Kimmel, Richard J. *Ghosts of Central New Jersey: Bizarre, Strange, and Deadly*. Atglen, PA: Schiffer Publishing, 2010.

Martinelli, Patricia A., and Charles A. Stansfield Jr. *Haunted New Jersey: Ghosts and Strange Phenomena of the Garden State*. Mechanicsburg, PA: Stackpole Books, 2004.

McCloy, James F., and Ray Miller Jr. *The Jersey Devil*. Moorestown, NJ: Middle Atlantic Press, 1976.

Meldrum, Charlotte. *Early Records of Cumberland County, New Jersey*. Westminster, MD: Willow Bend Books, 2001.

Moonsammy, Rita Zorn, David Steven Cohen, and Lorraine E. Williams, eds. *Pinelands Folklife*. New Brunswick, NJ: Rutgers University Press, 1987.

Mulford, William C. *Historical Tales of Cumberland County New Jersey*. Bridgeton, NJ: Evening News Company, n.d.

Nelson, William, ed. *Documents Relating to the Colonial History of the State of New Jersey*. Vol. 28. Paterson, NJ: Call Printing and Publishing, 1916.

New Jersey Bureau of Statistics and Records. *The Industrial Directory of New Jersey*. Paterson, NJ: News Printing, 1918.

New Jersey Municipal Data Book 2009. Woodside, CA: Information Publications, 2009.

Pepper, Adeline. *The Glass Gaffers of New Jersey and Their Creations from 1739 to the Present*. New York: Charles Scribner's Sons, 1971.

Pierce, John E. *Heart of the Pines: Ghostly Voices of the Pine Barrens*. Rev. ed. Hammonton, NJ: Batsto Citizens Committee, 2000.

Radko, Thomas R., ed. *Discovering New Jersey*. New Brunswick, NJ: Rutgers University Press, 1982.

Roberts, Russell. *Discover the Hidden New Jersey*. New Brunswick, NJ: Rutgers University Press, 1995.

Ross, Peter, and Fenwick Y. Hedley. *The New Jersey Coast in Three Centuries: History of the New Jersey Coast with Genealogical and Historic-Bibliographic Appendix*. Lewis Publishing, 1902.

Salter, Edwin. *Salter's History of Monmouth and Ocean Counties*. 1890; reprint, Westminster, MD: Heritage Books, 2007.

Sarver, Patrick. *New Jersey Day Trips*. New Brunswick, NJ: Rutgers University Press, 2007.

Sears, Charles. *The North American Phalanx, an Historical and Descriptive Sketch*. Prescott, WI: John M. Pryse, 1886.

Sokolow, Jayme A. *The North American Phalanx: A Nineteenth-Century Utopian Community*. Lewiston, NY: Mellen Press, 2009.

Stansfield, Charles A., Jr. *Haunted Jersey Shore: Ghosts and Strange Phenomena of the Garden State Coast*. Mechanicsburg, PA: Stackpole Books, 2006.

Stewart, Frank H. *Notes on Old Gloucester County New Jersey*. Vol. 2. Woodbury, NJ: Constitution Company, 1934.

Stockton, Frank R. *Stories of New Jersey*. New Brunswick, NJ: Rutgers University Press, 1961.

Swing, Gilbert S. *Events in the Life and History of the Swing Family*. Camden, NJ: Graw, Garrigues & Graw, 1889.

Tassin, Susan Hutchison. *Pennsylvania Ghost Towns: Uncovering the Hidden Past*. Mechanicsburg, PA: Stackpole Books, 2007.

Trapani, Bob Jr. *Lighthouses of New Jersey-Delaware: History, Mystery, Legends, and Lore*. Elkton, MD: Myst and Lace, 2005.

Tuttle, Hudson, and James M. Peebles. *The Year-Book of Spiritualism for 1871*. Boston: William White, 1871.

Weygandt, Cornelius. *Down Jersey: Folks and Their Jobs, Pine Barrens, Salt Marsh, and Sea Islands*. New York: D. Appleton-Century, 1940.

Online Sources

"Andover Township History." *Andover Township*. Retrieved December 11, 2010. www.andovertwp.org/history.htm.

"Barnegat Light, New Jersey." *Barnegat Light*. Retrieved September 15, 2010. http:/barnegatlight.org/past.html.

"Batsto Village: 1890." *Brian and Kim's Genealogy Page*. Retrieved April 22, 2011. http://freepages.genealogy.rootsweb.ancestry.com/~batsto.

Brown, Deneen. "Excavation of Sites Such as Timbuctoo, N.J., Is Helping to Rewrite African American History." *Washington Post*. Retrieved March 19, 2011. www.washingtonpost.com/wp-dyn/content/article/2010/08/02/AR2010080205217.html.

Carhart, Lowell. "Cemeteries: Topanemus Burying Ground: Freehold, Monmouth Co., NJ." *USGenWeb Archives*. Retrieved March 9, 2011. www.files.usgwarchives.net/nj/monmouth/cemetery/topanemus01.txt.

"Deserted Village/Feltville." *Mountainside Public Library Local History Collection*. Retrieved April 1, 2011. www.mountainsidelibrary.org/HistoryFiles/DavidFelt.pdf.

"Estellville Glassworks." *South Jersey Forevergreen*. Retrieved April 2, 2011. ww.forevergreennj.com/C/Heritage_Sites/27/U/Estellville_Glassworks/250.asp x.

Fox, Karen. "Whalers: The Link to Our Past." *Cape May*. Retrieved October 9, 2010. http:/capemay.com/magazine/2009/11/whalers-the-link-to-our-past.

"George Stiles v. Daniel Richardson. Philadelphia. 1797–99." *Historical Society of Pennsylvania*. Retrieved March 29, 2011. www.hsp.org/default.aspx?id=1159.

"History of Aura: Located in Elk Township, New Jersey." *Welcome to Elk Township*. Retrieved March 1, 2011. www.elktownship.com/aura .html.

"The History of Branchville Borough." *Branchville, New Jersey: USA*. Retrieved September 8, 2010. www.branchville-nj.com.

"History of the Aura Methodist Church." *Welcome to Elk Township*. Retrieved March 1, 2011. www.elktownship.com/hamc.html.

"The History of Whitesbog." *Whitesbog Village*. Retrieved April 7, 2011. www.whitesbog.org/whitesboghistory/history1.htm.

"In the Name of Christ: Sowing, GROWing, and Serving." *Pittsgrove Presbyterian Church*. Retrieved April 2, 2011. www.daretownpres.org/OldChurch.

Jaquett, Josephine, and Elmer VanName. "Place Names of Salem County N.J." *West Jersey History Project*. Retrieved November 4, 2010. www.westjerseyhistory.org/books/salemnames.

Livio, Susan K. "Ancora Psychiatric Hospital faces federal investigation." *New Jersey Real-Time News*. Retrieved February 28, 2011. www.nj .com/news/index.ssf/2008/09/ancora_psychiatric_hospital_fa.html.

"Marlboro Municipal Records." *New Jersey's Monmouth County*. Retrieved March 29, 2011. www.visitmonmouth.com/page.aspx?Id=2645.

Nickles, Ann, and Joseph Henry Bennett. "Scullville." *Scullville*. Retrieved March 23, 2011. www.eht.com/history/Sketches/scullville/index.htm.

"North American Phalanx Records, 1841–1972." *Monmouth County Historical Association*. Retrieved February 1, 2011. www.monmouthhistory.org/Sections-read-20.html.

"Our History: 100 Years of Hope, Help, Healing." *Carrier Clinic*. Retrieved January 7, 2011. www.carrierclinic.org/history.php.

"Recovering Raritan Landing: The Archaeology of a Forgotten Town." *Raritan Landing*. Retrieved January 19, 2011. www.raritanlanding .com.

"Rockleigh History." *The Official Website of the Borough of Rockleigh*. Retrieved March 22, 2011. www.rockleighnj.org/history.

Six, Janet. "Hidden History of Ralston Heights." *Archaeology*. Retrieved December 4, 2010. www.archaeology.org/0405/abstracts/ralston.html.

Spahr, Rob. "Save Our Ghost Town: Residents want Township to Preserve Remnants of Abandoned Village, Factory." *Press of Atlantic City*. Retrieved February 11, 2011. www.pressofatlanticcity.com/news/press/ atlantic/article_1e8d4d0f-0c69-58aa-9d63-e64d275eeb4.html.

Trainor, Joseph, ed. "Crop Circles Appear in Rural New Jersey." *UFO Roundup*. Retrieved April 19, 2011. www.ufoinfo.com/roundup/v08/ md0821.shtml.

"Welcome to New Bridge Landing." *Historic New Bridge Landing Park Commission*. Retrieved January 29, 2011. www.newbridgelanding.org.

Wieczorek, Scott. "The Story of Pasadena and its Neighboring Clay Industry." *NJPineBarrens*. Retrieved May 5, 2011. www.njpinebarrens.com/ 2007/01/18/the-story-of-pasadena-and-its-neighboring-clay-industry.

INDEX